Also by Bruce Biggs:

Maori Marriage
The Structure of New Zealand Maaori
English–Maori Dictionary
Selected Readings in Maori (with P. Hohepa and S. M. Mead)
Selected Readings in Maori Literature (with Chris Lane and Helen Cullen)
Complete English–Maori Dictionary
English–Maori Maori–English Dictionary
Nga Iwi o Tainui: The Traditional History of the Tainui People (ed.)
Cook Islands Maori Dictionary (ed.)
He Whiriwhiringa: Selected Readings in Maori (ed.)

let's learn
Maori

A Guide to the Study of the Maori Language

BRUCE BIGGS

AUCKLAND UNIVERSITY PRESS

To my son John Matengaro who wants to study Maori

First published by Bruce Biggs 1969
Revised edition 1973
Reprinted 1974, 1986, 1989, 1991, 1992, 1996

This edition published 1998 by Auckland University Press,
University of Auckland, Private Bag 92019, Auckland.
http://www.auckland.ac.nz/aup
Reprinted 2001

ISBN 1 86940 186 7

Printed by Publishing Press Ltd, Auckland

Contents

Introduction

Let's Learn Maori is a self-help tutor designed to facilitate study of the Polynesian language still spoken natively in those areas of New Zealand where Maoris form a significant proportion of the population. It should be used in conjunction with Williams's *Dictionary of the Maori Language* and *English–Maori Maori–English Dictionary* by the present author.

The set of cassettes specially planned to accompany this tutor, and containing most of the sentence examples from it, should also be used if at all possible. For those without access to the recordings a brief pronunciation guide is appended; but it should be realised that any written guide to pronunciation runs a poor second to the voice of a native speaker.

It is not claimed that *Let's Learn Maori* will make learning easy. Any language is a highly complicated symbolic system in which reasonable competence is acquired only after prolonged and serious study. No books, or records, or combination of both will alter that. It *is* claimed however that the analysis of Maori presented here has proved to be a helpful learning and teaching aid over the past twenty years, especially to those who incline towards a systematic rather than an anecdotal approach.

The tutor endeavours to present a complete description of the structure of simple sentences together with a few more complex sentence types. It emphasises and explains grammatical features which differ from English and supplies sentence examples for each structure it describes. Extensive cross-referencing is included and a combined index, vocabulary and glossary of grammatical terms is provided. The recordings provide an oral–aural tutor matched to the written exposition. Used in conjunction the tutor and recordings should enable the student to reach a reasonable standard in the four language skills, reading, writing, speaking, and hearing with understanding.

Maori, like all Polynesian languages, has phonemically distinctive vowel length, and a great many words are distinguished solely by pronouncing a given vowel as short or long. The conventional orthography, devised by English-speaking missionaries, failed to take this into account. Long vowels were not distinguished from short vowels, and reading involved a good deal of guesswork. It is now generally recognised that it is essential to mark vowel length by some method if such meanings as 'parrot', 'red-hot', 'clothing' (all written *kaka* in the conventional orthography) are to be distinguished.

Williams's Maori Dictionary, in citation forms only, marks phonemically long vowels by means of a macron, thus *kākā* 'parrot', *kakā* 'red-hot', *kaka* 'clothing'. In *Let's Learn Maori*, and in *English–Maori Maori–English Dictionary*, all long vowels are doubled, thus *kaakaa* 'parrot', *kakaa* 'red-hot', *kaka* 'clothing'. The doubling of the vowel means simply that it is lengthened. No rearticulation of the vowel is indicated.

Reading practice in the double-vowel orthography used in the tutor may be obtained with *He Whiriwhiringa: Selected Readings in Maori* (AUP, 1997), a collection chosen by Patrick W. Hohepa, Sidney M. Mead, and the present author. Aural–oral competence should be improved by taking every opportunity to hear spoken Maori, and in turn, to speak Maori. Tape-recorders are a boon in this respect, enabling one to build up a collection of spoken material, and to check one's own competence in speaking.

The text of the tutor is arranged in 54 sections, most of which have subsections, or even sub-subsections. The sections are numbered in digit figures, subsections are indicated by a first decimal point, and sub-subsections by two decimal points, so 23.12 indicates a subsection of 23.1 which is a subsection of 23. To facilitate the location of references all of the sections to be found on any two facing pages are indicated by the numbers at the top left and right corners of the pages. All index references and cross-references are given in terms of section numbers rather than page numbers.

The combined index and vocabulary contains glosses for all Maori words used in the tutor, as well as full and detailed indexing of grammatical and phonological points covered. It should be understood that the glosses of Maori words given in the index are not intended to cover all, or even the greater part, of the meaning of such words. Williams's Maori Dictionary should be consulted for complete information.

All Maori words are printed in italic type. The only exception to this rule concerns the use in English text of Maori words which are generally recognised as being part of the vocabulary of New Zealand English. Such words, Maori for example, are spelt conventionally, and do not show the quantity of vowels. The same word would appear in Maori text as *Maaori*.

English text is printed in Roman type. In running text the English translation of Maori examples is marked off by single raised commas, e.g. *Te Tangata* 'the man' is a nominal phrase.

1. The phrase

1.1 The phrase as a pause unit of speech

(The examples in this section may be heard on Track 2 of the recordings.)

The phrase, not the word, is the unit of Maori speech which must be emphasised in learning. It is the natural grammatical unit of the language, and even more importantly, it is the natural pause unit of speech. Every sentence in Maori consists of one or more phrases. After every phrase it is permissible to pause briefly. On the other hand it is incorrect to pause after each word within a phrase.

To a native speaker of Maori the pause points come naturally. For our purposes, however, it will be helpful if phrases are marked off by commas, thus:

Haere mai, ki te whare.
Come to the house.

Ka pai, te whare nei.
This house is good.

Each phrase is said as a single intonation contour, the voice rising to a point of intensity which is called the phrase stress. The position of the phrase stress will vary from phrase to phrase, and it may shift position in the same phrase, according to that phrase's position in the sentence. Rules to determine the position of phrase stress are given in section 54.6. In the following examples phrase stress is marked by an acute accent. Elsewhere an appropriate positioning of phrase stress may be determined by listening carefully to the recording of the sentence concerned.

Haere mái, ki te wháre.
Come to the house.

Ka pái, te wháre nei.
This house is good.

Teenáa koe, Ráapata.
Good-day friend.

3

Kei héa, too káainga?
Where is your home?

Kei Aakarána, tooku káainga.
My home is in Auckland.

Listen carefully to the recording of Track 2 until you can recognise the sound of phrase stress. Throughout the recordings each example will be said twice, then followed by a pause which will allow you to repeat it twice. Imitate the pronunciation carefully, paying special attention to phrase stress and to the flow and intonation of the instructor's voice.

1.2   The grammar of the phrase

A Maori phrase consists of two parts, a nucleus and a periphery. The nucleus may be thought of as the central part of the phrase, containing its lexical meaning. The periphery is that part of the phrase which precedes and follows the nucleus. The periphery of the phrase contains its grammatical meaning, indicating, for example, whether it is singular or plural, verbal or nominal, past or present, and so on. A phrase will always contain a nucleus. In some phrases there will be a word or words preceding the nucleus, in other phrases there will be a word or words following the nucleus, while in many phrases there will be words both preceding and following. In a few cases the nucleus will stand alone. The position preceding the nucleus of a phrase is called the preposed periphery; the position following the nucleus is called the postposed periphery.

Maori words may be classified into two kinds, bases and particles. Bases express lexical or real meaning. Thus the words *whare* 'house' and *pai* 'good' are bases. On the other hand *ka* is a particle. It occurs in the preposed periphery and indicates that the following base is being used verbally, so we may say that its meaning is grammatical rather than lexical. Some particles indicate grammatical relationships and functions such as subject, predicate, comment, and focus (see 38 for definition and discussion of these terms). Other particles, especially those occurring in the postposed periphery, limit and define (qualify) the meaning of the base in the nucleus. Bases always occur in the nucleus of the phrase, while particles, with certain exceptions, occur in the periphery.

PREPOSED PERIPHERY	NUCLEUS	POSTPOSED PERIPHERY
ka	pai	
te	whare	nei
	haere	mai
ki te	whare	
kei	hea	
to	kaainga	
kei	Aakarana	
tooku	kaainga	

In the first of the phrases in the above table, the base *pai* meaning 'good' is shown to be used verbally by the presence of the verbal particle *ka* in the periphery. So the phrase may be translated 'is good'. In the second phrase the nucleus contains the base *whare* 'house'. In the preposed periphery the particle *te* indicates that 'the (one)' house is being referred to. In the postposed periphery *nei* indicates 'proximity to the speaker', so the whole phrase may be translated 'this house'.

In the third phrase the base *haere* has a range of meaning which covers both of the English words 'come' and 'go'. In the postposed periphery, however, the particle *mai* 'motion towards speaker' indicates that in this case *haere* should be translated 'come', and the whole phrase has the meaning 'come hither' or 'come here'.

In the fourth phrase the base *whare* appears again in the nucleus position. In the preposed periphery we find two particles. *Ki* indicates 'motion towards' and, as we know, *te* means 'the (one)'. The phrase may be translated, therefore, 'to the house'.

In the fifth phrase the base *hea* 'where?' is preceded by the preposed particle *kei* which means 'present position'. The sixth phrase contains the base *kaainga* 'home' preceded by the particle *to* 'your'. Literally the two phrases mean 'at where your home?' or 'where is your home?'

In the seventh and eighth phrases the base *Aakarana* 'Auckland' is preceded by the same particle *kei* 'present position' and the base *kaainga* 'home' is preceded by *tooku* 'my'. The sentence therefore means 'my home is at Auckland.'

All Maori phrases are either verbal phrases or nominal phrases. A verbal phrase is marked as such by a preposed verbal particle as in *ka pai,* or by imperative intonation as in *haere mai!* (see 8 for discussion of verbal particles). Certain postposed particles may also mark a phrase as being verbal (23.22–3). Any phrase which is not a verbal phrase is a nominal phrase.

Nominal phrases:

ki te whare	to the house
te whare	the house
kei hea?	where?
kei Aakarana	at Auckland
to kaainga	your home
tooku kaainga	my home

Verbal phrases:

ka pai	(it is) good
haere mai!	come here!

2. The articles

2.1 The indefinite article *he*

The indefinite article *he* is preposed to bases which are being used nominally and indefinitely. Number is not indicated by the indefinite article so *he whare* may mean 'a house' or 'some houses'. Notice that the Maori equivalents of English mass nouns (flesh, water, corn, milk, money, etc.) can occur with *he*. In such cases *he* will always translate as 'some'. So we get *he kiko, he wai, he kaanga, he miraka, he moni,* 'some flesh, some water, some corn, some milk, some money'. *He* almost always occurs at the beginning of the phrase in which it occurs, and a phrase containing *he* is identified as an indefinite nominal phrase.

He taane
a man, some men

he kootiro
a girl, some girls

he kaainga
a village, some villages

he aaporo
an apple, some apples

2.2 The definite articles *te* and *nga*

2.21 *Te* is singular, *nga* is plural

Te and *nga* are definite articles which are preposed to bases being used nominally. *Te* indicates that the base is in the singular number; *nga* indicates plural number. A phrase which begins with *te* or *nga* is a definite nominal phrase.

te whare	nga whare
the house	the houses

te taane	*nga taane*
the man	the men
te kootiro	*nga kootiro*
the girl	the girls
te kaainga	*nga kaainga*
the village	the villages
te aaporo	*nga aaporo*
the apple	the apples
te kupu	*nga kupu*
the word	the words
te iwi	*nga iwi*
the tribe	the tribes
te tikanga	*nga tikanga*
the custom	the customs

2.22 *Te* as a class marker

When a whole class of objects is being referred to, the singular definite article *te* is often used instead of the plural definite article *nga*. So *te kereruu* might mean 'the (one) pigeon' or 'the (class of) pigeons' as when we say 'the pigeon is a beautiful bird'.

2.23 *Nga* with English mass nouns

It must not be thought that because a Maori word is the equivalent of one of the English mass nouns that it will not occur with *nga*. *Nga wai, nga moni, nga kaanga, nga kai, nga toto* 'water, money, corn, food, blood' are all appropriate Maori phrases in certain contexts.

2.3 The proper article *a*

Personal nouns, such as the names of people, or the names of animals or things which are personified, do not occur with the definite or indefinite articles, unless the article is an integral part of the name as in *Te Rauparaha,* for example. In such cases the form no longer fulfils its function as an article, and it should be regarded simply as part of the name. All personal nouns, in certain situations which will be defined later (35.1), are preposed by the proper article *a*. Examples of this are to be found at 5.4, 6.32 and 10.2. The proper article always begins the phrase in which it occurs, and any phrase containing the proper article is a proper nominal phrase.

Kei hea, a Pita?
Where is Peter?

Kei Aakarana, a Pita.
Peter is at Auckland.

Kei hea, a Te Rauparaha?
Where is Te Rauparaha?

Kei tooku kaainga, a Te Rauparaha.
Te Rauparaha is at my home.

Kei hea a Mere, a Hoani, a Tiaki?
Where are Mary, John and Jack?

Kei Aakarana, a Mere, kei Pooneke, a Hoani, kei Whakataane, a Tiaki.
Mary is at Auckland, John is at Wellington, Jack is at Whakatane.

Ka pai, a Matiu; ka kino, a Ruka.
Matthew is good; Luke is bad.

Ka pai, teenei whare, a Tama-te-kapua.
This house Tama-te-kapua is good.

Ka kino, teeraa whare, a Maru poo.
That house Maru poo is bad.

3. The positional particles *nei, na, ra* and the definitives *teenei, teenaa, teeraa*

3.1 *Nei, na* and *ra* postposed to bases

The particles *nei, na* and *ra* can be postposed to a base to indicate position near the speaker (*nei*), position near the person spoken to (*na*), and position distant from both (*ra*). In translating such phrases 'here, there' or 'this, that, these, those' are appropriate.

> *te pune nei*
> the spoon here, this spoon
>
> *nga pune nei*
> the spoons here, these spoons
>
> *te kapu ra*
> the cup (yonder), that cup
>
> *nga whare na*
> the houses there (near you), those houses
>
> *te whare ra*
> the house (yonder), that house

3.2 Pronunciation of *na* and *ra*

Na and *ra* are pronounced short before a full-stop and long elsewhere. As with other particles which alternate between short and long these two are always written short.

3.3 *Nei, na* and *ra* combined with the definite article

The positional particles may also be affixed to the definite article *te* to form a set of definitives (15). (Note that the *e* of *te* and the *a* of *na* and *ra* become long.) *Teenei* 'this', *teenaa* 'that (near you)', *teeraa* 'that (yonder)'. Definitives are preposed to bases, as in the following examples:

teenei pereti
this plate

teenaa pereti
this plate (near you)

teeraa kaapata
that cupboard (yonder)

There is little, if any, difference in meaning between *teenei teepu* and *te teepu nei,* both indicating 'one definite table near the speaker', hence 'this table'. The choice of one form rather than another can be regarded as optional.

To indicate plural number all definitives drop the initial *t-,* thus:

eenei naihi
these knives

eenaa tuuru
those chairs

eeraa hoopane
those pots

To summarise the previous paragraphs study the following examples carefully.

te teepu nei or *teenei teepu*
this table

nga teepu nei or *eenei teepu*
these tables

te naihi na or *teenaa naihi*
that knife (near you)

nga naihi na or *eenaa naihi*
those knives (near you)

te paoka ra or *teeraa paoka*
that fork (yonder)

nga paoka ra or *eeraa paoka*
those forks (yonder)

Kei hea, teeraa naihi? or *kei hea, te naihi ra?*
Where is that knife?

Kei hea, eeraa naihi? or *kei hea, nga naihi ra?*
Where are those knives?

Kei tooku kaainga, teeraa pereti or *kei tooku kaainga, te pereti ra.*
That plate is at my home.

Kei tooku kaainga, eeraa pereti or *kei tooku kaainga, nga pereti ra.*
Those plates are at my home.

Ka pai, teenaa tuuru or *ka pai, te tuuru na.*
That chair is good.

Ka pai, eenaa tuuru or *ka pai, nga tuuru na.*
Those chairs are good.

Kei Aakarana, teeraa kootiro or *kei Aakarana, te kootiro ra.*
That girl is at Auckland.

Kei Aakarana, eeraa kootiro or *kei Aakarana, nga kootiro ra.*
Those girls are at Auckland.

Haere mai, ki teenei whare or *haere mai, ki te whare nei.*
Come to this house.

Haere mai, ki eenei whare or *haere mai, ki nga whare nei.*
Come to these houses.

4. Nominal sentences

(The examples in this section may be heard on Tracks 3 & 4 of the recordings.)

4.1 Indefinite phrase and common definite phrase

As mentioned previously (2.1) we distinguish verbal phrases, which usually begin with a verbal particle, e.g. *ka pai*, from nominal phrases. Nominal phrases usually begin with a definitive (15), e.g. *te whare*, or a preposition (17), e.g. *ki te whare*.

Phrases combine to build sentences and, unexpectedly to speakers of English, many Maori sentences consist of two nominal phrases juxtaposed. Such verbless, or nominal sentences often correspond to English sentences containing the verb 'to be'. The sentence 'this fish is a snapper' is translated by the Maori nominal sentence *he taamure, teenei ika*.

Any sentence is a predication in which something is said about something. The thing being discussed is called the subject. What is said about the subject is called the predicate. In the English sentence quoted above 'this fish' is the subject and 'is a snapper' is the predicate. As is usual in English the subject precedes the predicate. English uses a part of the verb 'to be' but Maori makes the same statement by juxtaposing two nominal phrases to give us *he taamure, teenei ika*. In contrast to English the Maori subject (*teenei ika*) follows the predicate (*he taamure*).

Here are further examples of 'indefinite nominal sentences' which are so-named because they begin with the indefinite article.

He aha teenei?
What is this?

He mere, te mea nei.
This thing is a greenstone club.

He paipera, teenei pukapuka.
This book is a bible.

He rangatira, teeraa tangata.
That man is a chief.

He taariana, te hooiho.
The horse is a stallion.

He kereruu, nga manu ra.
Those birds are pigeons.

Many Maori phrases that require translation by English adjectival predicates are used in these indefinite nominal sentences.

He aataahua, nga kootiro.
The girls are beautiful.

He pai, te koorero.
The talk is good.

He pirau, nga kuumara.
The sweet-potatoes are rotten.

He kino, teeraa tikanga.
That custom is evil.

Finally it should be noted that although, in translation, the use of the English verb 'to be' requires the selection of a tense, the Maori sentences are tenseless. The last sentence, for example, might equally well be translated 'that custom was evil'.

4.2 Indefinite phrase and proper name

If, in a nominal sentence, the second phrase contains a proper name, either the name of a person or a place, it will take the preposed proper article *a*, as in *he rangatira, a Tamahae*, 'Tamahae is a chief'. This is in accordance with the rule that a proper name standing as subject takes the proper article (35.1).

He aha, a Maarama?
What is Maarama?

He kootiro, a Maarama.
Maarama is a girl.

He aha, a Pooneke?
What is Wellington?

He taaone, a Pooneke.
Wellington is a town.

He maunga, a Pirongia.
Pirongia is a mountain.

He roto, a Waikare-moana.
Waikare-moana is a lake.

He awa, a Whanganui.
Whanganui is a river.

He maania, a Kaingaroa.
Kaingaroa is a plain.

He kootiro aataahua, a Maarama.
Maarama is a beautiful girl.

He taaone nui, a Pooneke.
Wellington is a big town.

He maunga teitei, a Taranaki.
Mt Egmont is a lofty mountain.

He awa tere, a Whanganui.
Whanganui is a swift river.

He maania roa, a Kaingaroa.
Kaingaroa is a long plain.

Note that in the last five examples there occur compound phrases containing two bases. In such cases the second base always describes, or further defines, the meaning of the first base. In traditional terms we may say that the adjective in Maori follows the noun it describes.

4.3   Two definite phrases

A nominal sentence may consist of two definite nominal phrases, that is, two phrases each of which contains a definitive (15). The second phrase will usually be a compound phrase containing two bases. In these cases,

4.3

where a definite nominal phrase begins the sentence, correct Maori requires that the focus-marking particle *ko* (38.3) be preposed as in *ko te taariana te hoiho tere* 'the stallion is the fast horse'; but in fast or informal speech *ko* is often omitted.

Ko te aha teenei?
What is this?

Ko te hooro teenei.
This is the hall.

Ko te hooro, te whare pikitia.
The hall is (used as) the cinema.

Ko te kura, te whare kanikani.
The school is (used as) the dancehall.

Ko te kauri, te raakau nui.
The kauri is the (really) big tree.

4.4   Proper name plus definite phrase

If the first phrase of a nominal sentence contains a proper name, it too must begin with *ko,* and not with the proper article *a.*

Ko wai te rangatira?
Who is the chief?

Ko Turi, te rangatira.
Turi is the chief.

Ko Peta, te kaumaatua.
Peta is the respected elder.

Ko Maarama, te kootiro aataahua.
Maarama is the beautiful girl.

Ko Tamahae, te toa.
Tamahae is the warrior.

Ko Maru, te tohunga.
Maru is the priest.

Ko Pita, te kuramaahita.
Pita is the schoolmaster.

Ko Tama-te-kapua, teeraa whare.
That house (yonder) is Tama-te-kapua.

Ko tooku kaainga, teenei whare.
This house is my home.

Ko Aakarana, teenei.
This is Auckland.

Ko Maaui-pootiki, teenei tamaiti.
This child is Maaui-Pootiki.

Ko teenei whare, te whare pai.
This house is the good one.

4.5   Subject in focus

In a nominal sentence a phrase beginning with the indefinite article *he* is always the predicate, and as we have seen, the predicate usually precedes the subject in a Maori sentence. However, in order to emphasise the subject of a sentence it may be put before the predicate. Instead of *he maunga a Pirongia* 'Pirongia is a mountain' we may find *ko Pirongia he maunga* 'Pirongia is a mountain'.

In such sentences the subject is said to be in focus, or focused (38.31). Notice that the proper article *a* which precedes proper nouns as subject after the predicate is replaced by *ko* 'focus preposition' when the subject is in focus.

5. Active and stative verbal sentences

(The examples in this section may be heard on Track 5 of the recordings.)

5.1 Active sentences

Consider the following sentence: *ka tangi, te tamaiti* 'the child weeps'. It begins with a verbal phrase, so defined by the verbal particle *ka* in the preposed periphery. The nucleus of the phrase is a base of the class called universal (see 16.3). This is followed by a nominal phrase introduced by the singular definite article. The verbal phrase expresses an action, the nominal phrase tells who or what performed the action. This is the usual, though not invariable order in a Maori sentence; predicate first, followed by subject. (See 38 for definition of subject and predicate.) In English it is more usual for the reverse order to be found, as in 'the child weeps'.

It should be noted that the verbal particle *ka* has no time significance. It simply marks its phrase as verbal and as the predicate of the sentence. Since English demands the selection of a time-marking tense, the present tense has been chosen to translate the Maori examples.

Ka kai, te rangatira.
The chief eats.

Ka inu, te hooiho.
The horse drinks.

Ka oma, te kootiro.
The girl runs.

Ka haere, te wahine.
The woman goes.

Ka karanga, te kuia.
The old woman calls.

5.2 Stative sentences

In 5.1 we saw that a verbal phrase containing a universal base, followed by a definite nominal phrase, formed an action-actor sentence, thus: *ka tangi, te tamaiti,* 'the child weeps'.

There is another class of bases called statives (discussed in 16.4). A verbal phrase containing a stative and followed by a nominal phrase forms a sentence in which the first phrase expresses a state, condition or attribute of whatever is expressed in the second phrase. Thus, *ka tika, te koorero* 'the talk is correct'. Again the nominal phrase is the subject of the sentence and the verbal phrase is predicate.

5.3 Pronunciation of *ka*

When listening to the recording of the examples in this lesson notice that if the rest of the phrase beginning with *ka* contains no more than two vowels, *ka* will be pronounced with a long vowel; but if the remainder of the phrase contains more than two vowels *ka* will be pronounced short. It would be inconvenient to spell *ka* sometimes with one *a* and sometimes with two, and it is unnecessary because the rule given above will always indicate the correct pronunciation.

Ka poouri, te wahine.
The woman is sad.

Ka pai, teenei koorero.
This talk is good.

Ka roa, te haere.
The journey is long.

Ka mate, te wahine.
The woman is ill (or dead).

Ka pai, teenei.
This is good.

Ka nui, te pai.
Very good. (The goodness is great.)

Ka puuhae, te wahine.
The woman is jealous.

Ka mutu, te koorero.
The talk is finished (ended).

Ka oti, te mahi.
The work is finished (completed).

Ka pau, te kaha.
The strength is finished (exhausted).

5.4   Personal names as subject

If the subject phrase in an active or a stative sentence contains a personal name it will be preposed by the proper article *a:*

Ka kai a Pita.
Peter eats.

Ka inu a Maarama.
Maarama drinks.

Ka haere, a Tamahae.
Tamahae goes.

Ka puuhae, a Toro.
Toro is jealous.

Ka mate, a Kura.
Kura is ill.

Ka ora, a Rangi.
Rangi is well.

Ka kata a Kae.
Kae laughs. (Said of a person who is hard to make laugh. Kae had good reason not to laugh. When he did he was recognised by his crooked teeth as the killer of Tutunui, Tinirau's pet whale. That laugh was the death of Kae.)

5.41   Dialectal note
Some North Auckland speakers of Maori do not use the proper article *a* before a personal name used as subject of the sentence. It is not known whether this usage is modern or traditional in the area.

6. Comments introduced by *i* and *ki*

6.1 General

Active and stative verbal sentences containing two phrases may be expanded by a phrase beginning with either *i* or *ki*. Such an expansion is called a comment (see 38.4 for definition and discussion). Comments beginning with *ki* can always be regarded as the goal, in a broad sense, of the predicate, since the basic meaning of *ki* is 'motion towards'. Thus:

Ka haere atu te wahine ki te taaone.
The woman goes away to town.

Ka whakarongo te tangata ki te manu.
The man listens to the bird.

Ka rite teenei ki teenaa.
This is equal to that.

A comment beginning with *i* following a predicate containing a universal class base (i.e. in an active sentence) can also be regarded as the goal of the predicate: *Ka patu te tangata i te kurii* 'the man beats the dog'. But in the case of a stative sentence a comment beginning with *i* marks the cause or agent of the predicate and can usually be translated 'by'.

Ka oti te mahi i nga kaimahi.
The work is completed by the workers.

Ka hoohaa te whaea i nga tamariki.
The mother was impatient with (sick of) the children.

Ka mate teenei tangata i teenaa tangata.
This man was beaten by that man.

After both universal and stative predicates a comment in *i* may also indicate location in place of time, according to context.

Ka haere te ope i te ahiahi.
The party went in the evening.

6.1

Ka hinga te raakau i te ngahere.
The tree fell in the forest.

Comments beginning with *i* and *ki* are discussed more fully in the following sections.

6.2   Comments beginning with *ki* 'motion towards'

(All examples in this section may be heard on Track 6 of the recordings.)

In both active and stative sentences (5.1 and 5.2) where the verbal phrase indicates motion towards a goal the comment will begin with *ki*. The motion may be actual, as with *haere,* or figurative, as with *titiro* 'look', or *hiahia* 'desire, yearn for' and other words expressive of emotion. Notice in the examples that follow, that if the English translation employs an intransitive verb an appropriate preposition will also be needed. It would be unwise, however, to equate *ki* with any one English preposition. It should be regarded as having a very broad meaning which embraces the general idea of motion towards a goal.

Ka haere, te wahine, ki te whare.
The woman goes to the house.

Ka titiro, a Pita, ki te rangi.
Peter looks towards the sky.

Ka hinga, te raakau, ki te whenua.
The tree falls to the ground.

Ka rongo, te tangata, ki te waiata.
The man hears the song.

Ka koorero, te rangatira, ki te iwi.
The chief speaks to the tribe.

Ka piirangi, te tamaiti, ki te aarani.
The child wants the orange.

Ka whawhai, a Tamahae, ki te taniwha.
Tamahae fights the monster.

Ka whawhai, te taniwha, ki a Tamahae.
The monster fights Tamahae.

Ka aroha, te kuia, ki te tamaiti.
The old lady pities the child.

Ka hariruu, a Mere, ki a Rongo.
Mary shakes hands with Rongo.

6.21 *Ki* comments containing universals

If the comment beginning with *ki* contains a universal base preceded by the singular definite article *te,* it may be translated by an infinitive verb in English. It should be noted that in this construction the 'actor' of the comment in *ki* is always the same as the actor of the verbal phrase.

Ka tuu ake, te rangatira, ki te whaikoorero.
The chief stands up to speak.

Ka haere, eenei kootiro, ki te kaukau.
These girls go to bathe.

Ka haere, nga taitama, ki te whawhai.
The young men go to fight.

6.3 Comments beginning with *i* 'connective'

(Examples from this section may be heard on Track 7 of the recordings.)

In both active and stative sentences the comment will often begin with *i.* Where the base in the verbal phrase is a universal, it will be the goal (object) of the sentence; but where the verbal base is a stative the comment will be the actor or agent of the sentence. Compare the two sentences following. In the first *inu* 'drink' is a universal; in the second *ora* 'to be well, alive' is a stative.

Ka inu, te tangata, i te rongoa.
The man drinks the medicine.

Ka ora, te tangata, i te rongoa.
The man is made well by the medicine.

At this point it is clear that the distinction between universals and statives is a crucial one. Unfortunately the only way to tell one from the other is by meaning, which must be learned from the English gloss. Statives express qualities, states, and events that happen to one, e.g. *pai* 'to be good', *mate* 'to be ill, dead', *whaanau* 'to be born'. Universals express actions. Throughout this tutor statives and universals are carefully translated so that their class is obvious. Where necessary statives will be distinguished by S; and universals will have suffixed an appropriate passive suffix, e.g. *karanga-tia*.

6.31 Stative sentences with comments in *i*

Ka oti, te whare, i nga kaimahi.
The house was completed by the workers.

Ka hoohaa, nga rangatira, i teenaa koorero.
The chiefs are bored by that talk.

Ka koa, te iwi, i teeraa koorero.
The tribe is glad because of that talk.

Ka pai, te rangatira, i te piki kootuku.
The chief is made handsome by his white-heron plume.

Ka mate, te wahine, i te hiakai.
The woman is dying of hunger.

Ka mate, te tamaiti, i te whakamaa.
The child is ashamed.

Ka riro, te wahine, i te taane kee.
The woman is taken away by another man.

Ka mahue, a Mere, i te pahi.
Mary has been left by the bus.

Ka mataku, a Rewi, i te hooiho.
Rewi is frightened of the horse.

Ka hinga, te iwi nei, i a Hongi.
This tribe was defeated by Hongi.

Ka paru, te tamaiti, i te auahi.
The child is dirty with smoke.

6.32 Active sentences with comments in *i*

Ka hari, a Rewi, i te kiriimi.
Rewi carries the cream.

Ka puruma, a Tamahae, i te iaari.
Tamahae sweeps the yard.

Ka here, a Paka, i nga kurii.
Paka ties up the dogs.

Ka tuku, te heramana, i te haika.
The sailor lets go the anchor.

Ka tia, te kaapene, i te poti.
The captain steers the boat.

Ka hoko, te matua, i nga tiikiti.
The parent buys the tickets.

Ka whai, nga tamariki, i nga kaawhe.
The children chase the calves.

Ka tatari, a Mere, i te pahi.
Mary waits for the bus.

7. Passives

(The examples in this section may be heard on Track 8 of the recordings.)

7.1 Passive transforms of active sentences

Active sentences (i.e., sentences containing an active universal base in the verbal phrase) can be changed to passive sentences as in the following example:

Ka inu, te tangata, i te wai.
The man drinks the water.

Ka inumia, te wai, e te tangata.
The water is drunk by the man.

Such a change from one sentence type to a related sentence type may be called a transformation. In this case four steps are involved.

1. A passive suffix is added to the active universal base. *Inu* becomes *inumia.*

2. The particle *i* or *ki* introducing the comment which, in this case, is the goal of the sentence, is dropped. *Te wai* is now the subject of the sentence, since it is the unmarked nominal phrase (38.2)

3. The actor (agent) of the passive sentence is introduced by *e* the 'agentive particle'. *Te tangata* becomes *e te tangata*. This phrase is now the agentive comment of the sentence (38.4).

4. The two phrases which have changed function also switch order, but this change of order is optional. Instead of *ka inumia te wai e te tangata* we may have *ka inumia e te tangata te wai* though this order would be less usual.

7.2 Personal names in passive sentences

Ka aawhina a Pita i a Mere.
Pita helps Mere.

Ka aawhinatia a Mere e Pita.
Mere is helped by Pita.

In the active sentence the proper article is used before Pita which is a personal name used as subject of the sentence (5.4), and before Mere which is a personal name following a locative particle (11.6). In the passive sentence the proper article is retained before Mere, which is now the subject of the sentence, but lost before Pita, which is now neither subject of the sentence nor a personal name following a locative particle.

7.3   The shapes of the passive suffix

The passive suffix may take any of the following shapes: *-a, ia, -hia, -ina, -kia, -mia, -na, -nga, -ngia, -ria, -tia, -whia*. Although every universal base selects one of these alternative forms there is no rule which will determine the suffix appropriate to a particular base. For this reason the *English–Maori Maori–English Dictionary* lists each universal base with an appropriate passive suffix. Where a universal has a reduplicated first syllable (e.g., *tatari* 'wait') the first syllable is dropped and the vowel of the second syllable is usually lengthened (*taaria*); in certain other cases a short vowel of a diphthong is lengthened. The passive form of *whai* 'follow, pursue' is *whaaia*. All such cases are noted in *English–Maori Maori–English Dictionary*.

7.4   Examples

Ka haria, te kiriimi, e Rewi.
The cream is carried by Rewi.

Ka purumatia, te iaari, e Tamahae.
The yard is swept by Tamahae.

Ka herea, nga kurii, e Paka.
The dogs are tied up by Paka.

Ka tukua, te haika, e te heramana.
The anchor is let go by the sailor.

7.4

Ka tiaina, te poti, e te kaapene.
The boat is steered by the captain.

Ka hokona, nga tiikiti, e te matua.
The tickets are bought by the parent.

Ka whaaia, nga kaawhe, e nga tamariki.
The calves are chased by the children.

Ka tirohia, te moana, e Pita.
The sea is looked at by Peter.

Ka rongohia, te waiata, e te tangata.
The song is heard by the man.

Ka arohaina, te tamaiti, e te kuia.
The child is pitied by the old woman.

Ka taaria, te pahi, e Mere.
The bus is waited for by Mary.

I inumia, e Ngaamako, nga pua o te pohutukawa whakamarumaru.
The (nectar of) the flowers of the shady pohutukawa was drunk by
Ngaamako.

*Kua whaaia, a Tamahae, e te poaka tino nui. Ka whaaia hoki, te poaka, e
nga kurii.*
Tamahae was chased by the very big pig. And the pig was chased by the
dogs.

Ka puuhia, te poaka, e wai? Ka puuhia te poaka e Hata.
The pig was shot by whom? The pig was shot by Hata.

Ka utaina, te poaka, ki runga, i te hoiho. Ka tiikina atu, te hoiho, e Rewi.
The pig was loaded on the horse. The horse was fetched by Rewi.

8. Verbal particles

(Examples from this section may be heard on Track 9 of the recordings.)

8.1 General

We have already learned that actions and states are expressed by verbal phrases introduced by verbal particles; but we have used only the particle *ka*, which simply indicates that the phrase is verbal without saying anything about the time of the action or state. Most of the other verbal particles are also timeless, in fact only one, the 'past' particle *i*, unambiguously indicates time. All other verbal particles refer to the nature or aspect of the action or state denoted by the verbal phrase.

The verbal particles form a paradigm. One may be substituted for another to conjugate the verbal phrase, but no two verbal particles may occur together in the same phrase.

8.2 The paradigm of verbal particles

Following is the complete paradigm of verbal particles, with some indication of their meanings.

Ka	Inceptive	*Ka* has no specific reference to time though it is often used when the time is in fact future. It is always used when a new action is beginning. Hence the gloss 'inceptive'.
I	Past	Always indicates that the action is in the past.
Kua	Perfect	Indicates that the action is complete, usually in the fairly recent past.
Kia	Desiderative	Indicates that it would be desirable for something to occur, or exist. In a subordinate clause *kia* indicates purpose.
Me	Prescriptive	Indicates that something should or must be done.

E	Non-past	Action or state that is present or future. (See *e . . . ana* below.)
Kei	Warning	Translated by 'do not' or 'lest' (see 29).
Ina~ana	Punctative/ conditional	*Ina* occurs only in subordinate clauses. It indicates the point of time at which an action takes place, with the stipulation 'if it takes place.' Pedantically *ina* should be translated 'if and when' but in most contexts one of the two conjunctions will be more appropriate than the other. *Ana* is in free variation with *ina*.
E . . . ana	Imperfect	The combination of *e* 'non-past' and the postposed particle *ana* 'imperfect' indicates that the action or state is incomplete or continuous.

8.3   Examples

The translations of the following examples will help to illustrate the meanings of the various verbal particles. (Note that from this point on the practice of marking each and every phrase boundary by a comma is discontinued.)

Kua tae atu te waka ra, ki Hawaiki.
That canoe has reached Hawaiki.

I kitea e wai, teenei motu?
Who discovered this island? (This island was discovered by whom?)

Me hoki, te tamaiti ra, ki te kaainga.
That child must go home.

Ina tae te tangata ra ki taawaahi, ka mate ia.
When that man reaches the other side he will die.

Ka takoto te tamaiti, ka moe.
The child lay down and slept.

Ka mutu te kai, ka hui te iwi ra ki roto i te whare.
When the meal was over the people assembled in the house.

Kia tere!
Be quick!

Kia kaha, kia toa, kia manawanui!
Be strong, brave and steadfast.

Kia toru nga ika!
Let there be three fish.

Kia tapu toou ingoa.
Hallowed be thy name.

E haere ana te wahine, ki te moana.
The woman is going to the sea.

E moe ana te mata hii tuna, e ara ana te mata hii taua.
The eelfisher's eyes are sleeping, the warrior's eyes are awake.

Kia mate ururoa, kei mate tarakihi.
Die like a shark, not like a *tarakihi* (i.e. die fighting).

Kua whati te tara o te marama.
The horn of the moon is broken (said of a chief's death).

9. Personal pronouns

9.1 English and Maori pronominal systems contrasted

In English we distinguish three persons and two numbers in our pronouns (I, you, he; we, you, they). In Maori the pronouns distinguish four persons and three numbers. In English we distinguish subjective and objective cases (I, me; they, them) and sometimes gender (he, she; him, her). In Maori there is no distinction of case or gender.

9.2 Dual and plural numbers

In addition to plural pronouns Maori has a special set referring to two persons only. They are *taaua* and *maaua* 'we two' (see 9.3 for the difference between the two forms); *koorua* 'you two'; *raaua* 'they two'.

The plural forms are *taatou* and *maatou* 'we all' (see 9.3); *koutou* 'you all' and *raatou* 'they all'.

9.3 Inclusive and exclusive first person

In English we distinguish three persons. The extra person of the Maori pronomial system arises from the distinction between the first person 'we' which includes the person spoken to, and the 'we' which excludes the person spoken to. *Taaua* means 'we two, you and I' but *maaua* means 'we two, but not you', that is, 'someone else and I'. *Taatou* means 'we all, including you'; *maatou* means 'we all excluding you'. The terms inclusive and exclusive first person should now be clear.

E haere ana taaua, ki te taaone.
We two (you and I) are going to town.

E haere ana maaua, ki te taaone.
We two (not you) are going to town.

I tuutaki maatou, ki a Heta, i te taaone.
We (but not you) met Heta in town.

9.4 Table of personal pronouns

		FIRST PERSON INCLUSIVE	FIRST PERSON EXCLUSIVE	SECOND PERSON	THIRD PERSON
SINGULAR			*au, ahau* (I, me)	*koe* (you)	*ia* (he, she)
	DUAL	*taaua* (we, you and I)	*maaua* (we two, but not you)	*koorua* (you two)	*raaua* (they two)
	PLURAL	*taatou* (we all, including you)	*maatou* (we all, but not you)	*koutou* (you all)	*raatou* (they all)

9.5 Dialectal variation

In North Auckland the first person singular pronoun is usually *ahau,* and the second person dual is *kourua.*

On the East Coast the second person plural pronoun is *kootou.*

In all areas the forms *wau* and *awau* may be heard instead of *au, ahau* particularly after words ending in *o* or *u* (as *ko wau* 'it is I'), but the practice is not restricted to such positions.

10. Use of the personal pronouns

(Examples from this section may be heard on Track 10 of the recordings.)

10.1 Pronouns as subject of a sentence

Pronouns never occur with any of the common articles *te, nga, he,* and, unlike personal names, pronouns do not require the use of the personal article *a* when they stand as subject of a sentence.

I oma atu raatou!
They ran away.

E poowhiritia ana taatou.
We are being welcomed.

He rangatira ia, he ware ahau.
He is a chief, I am a commoner.

He waahine raatou, he taane taatou.
They are women, we are men.

10.2 Pronouns as comment in a sentence

When a pronoun (except *ahau)* follows any of the particles *kei, i, ki, hei,* it takes the proper article *a:*

E titiro ana ahau ki a ia.
I am looking at him.

I hariruu maatou ki a raatou.
We shook hands with them.

Kua mate koe i a au.
You have been beaten by me.

E whai ana maatou i a koutou.
We are chasing you.

10.3 Pronunciation note

Note that when the personal article precedes either of the pronouns *ia* or *koe* it is lengthened and takes the phrase stress. Notice also that while *ahau* never requires the personal article, its dialectal variant *au* does. *Au* preceded by *a* is pronounced *aau,* but written *a au.* This follows from the general rule of pronunciation, that adjacent like vowels in the same phrase are pronounced as a single long vowel. Remember to write *a au,* but pronounce *aau* in such sentences as *Haere mai ki a au!* 'come to me'.

10.4 Dialectal note

The practice of using the personal article *a* before the pronoun *ia* when it is a subject of the sentence, rare in early texts, is now widespread in colloquial Maori.

11. Locative particles *ki, kei, i, hei*

11.1 Position and meaning of the locative particles

The locative particles *ki, kei, i, hei,* of which we have already met *i* and *ki,* always occur at the beginning of a phrase. They have a common element of meaning in that each one indicates 'position in space or time'. A phrase beginning with any of these particles is called a comment (6, 38.4).

11.2 *Ki*

Ki has the basic meaning 'motion towards position in space or time'. It is often translated appropriately by 'to'.

> *E haere ana au, ki te whare miraka.*
> I am going *to* the milking shed.

11.3 *Kei*

Kei indicates 'present position'. It is often translated appropriately by 'at, on, with'.

> *Kei te whare-nui te tangata, inaianei.*
> The man is *at* the meeting house now.

11.4 *I*

I indicates 'position (usually) in the past'.

> *I te whare-nui te tangata, inanahi.*
> The man *was at* the meetinghouse yesterday.

11.5 *Hei*

Hei indicates 'position in the future'.

Hei te whare-nui te tangata, aapoopoo.
The man *will be at* the meeting-house tomorrow.

11.6 Personals after locative particles

A personal name or a pronoun (see 16.6 Personal Class Bases) which follows *ki, kei, i* or *hei* will take the personal article *a* (see 2.3). Notice that in such constructions an appropriate English translation will often use the verb 'to have'.

Kei a Pita te toki, inaianei.
Peter *has* the axe now.

I a Pita te toki, inanahi.
Peter *had* the axe yesterday.

Hei a Pita te toki, aapoopoo.
Peter *will have* the axe tomorrow.

I karanga atu, a Ani, ki a Arapeta
Anne called to Albert

11.7 Dialectal variation

In the Tuhoe–Bay of Plenty area, in the Taranaki–Wanganui River area, and on the East Coast, the forms *kei* and *hei* are replaced by *kai* and *hai.*

11.8 Examples

(Track 11 on the recordings.)

Kei te taha moana nga kootiro.
The girls are at the seaside.

I te ahiahi ka moe te kuia.
In the evening the old lady slept.

I te kaainga maatou, inapoo.
We were at home last night.

Hei te ata poo, ka hoki a Paania, ki te moana.
At dawn Paania will return to the sea.

I te ata ka tae maatou ki Te Reinga.
In the morning we arrived at Te Reinga.

Kei nga poo marama, e kitea ana a Rona me tana tahaa.
On moonlight nights Rona is seen with her calabash.

Ko Paania inaianei he koohatu kei raro i te moana e takoto ana.
Today Paania is a rock lying underneath the sea.

Kei roto i te keekee mauii he raawaru anake nga ika o reira.
Within (her) left armpit, only the fish called *raawaru* are there.

Kei te keekee matau he tamure anake nga ika o reira.
In her right armpit, snapper only are the fish of that place.

Kei waenganui o nga kuuhaa he haapuku anake nga ika o reira.
Between her thighs, *haapuku* alone are the fish of that place.

I teetahi ahiahi, ka haere a Tamahae ki te rapu tuna.
On a certain evening, Tamahae went to look for eels.

I te atapoo tonu, ka haere a Tamahae ki te whaiwhai poaka.
At early dawn Tamahae went pig-hunting.

I nga raa o mua, i noho te paapaka me te kooura ki te ngahere.
In days of yore, the crab and the crayfish lived in the forest.

I taua waa, ka tuu mai nga rangatira ki te koorero ki a ia.
At that time the chiefs stood forth to speak to him.

12. Locative bases

(Examples from this section may be heard on Track 12 of the recordings.)

12.1 Definition of locatives

Locative bases refer to position in space or time. They are distinguished grammatically by the fact that they never take a definite or an indefinite article, and unlike all other bases they can follow the locative particles *ki, kei, i, hei* directly, without any intervening particle.

Kei hea te rangatira?
Where is the chief?

Kei roto te rangatira i te whare-nui.
The chief is in the meeting-house.

Kei hea te pene?
Where is the pen?

Kei runga, te pene i te teepu.
The pen is on top of the table.

Kei raro te pene i te pukapuka.
The pen is under the book.

Kei hea te kurii?
Where is the dog?

Kei koo, kei tua i te whare.
Yonder, on the other side of the house.

Kei waho te kurii i te whare.
The dog is outside the house.

12.2 Common locatives

runga top, above	*raro* bottom, below
roto inside	*waho* outside

hea?, whea? where?	*konei* here
konaa there (near you)	*koraa* there (yonder)
mua front, before	*muri* back, behind, later
uta inland	*tai* seawards
taawaahi far side (river, sea)	*tua* far side (solid object)
waenganui middle	*reira* there, that place
taatahi seaside	*tahaki* aside

12.3 Place names

All place names are best regarded as locative bases, because place names, like locatives, can occur immediately after the locative particles.

Kei hea koutou e noho ana?
Where are you living?

Kei Pooneke maatou e noho ana.
We are living at Wellington.

If a place name normally occurs with a definite article, Te Kuiti for example, the article is an integral part of the name and will be retained when the place name occurs after a locative particle.

I hea raatou, inanahi?
Where were they yesterday?

I Te Kuiti raatou, inanahi.
They were at Te Kuiti yesterday.

12.4 Common idioms containing locatives

i muri iho
shortly afterwards

i mua noa atu
long ago

i konei tonu
right here

kei waenganui poo
in the middle of the night

ki roto
into

i roto
out of

12.5 Examples

I tae mai raatou ki Kaawhia.
They arrived at Kawhia.

Kei reira a Whatihua.
Whatihua is at that place.

Ka hoki te tangata ki uta.
The man went back inland.

Kua tae mai nga manuhiri ki konei.
The guests have arrived here.

Kua tomo atu raatou, ki roto i te whare.
They have entered into the house.

Kua puta mai raatou, i roto i te whare.
They have come out of the house.

13. Dominant and subordinate possession: the particles *a* and *o*

13.1 Distinction between dominant and subordinate possession

The preposed particles *a* and *o* always come at the beginning of a phrase. Both indicate possession, and both are translated by 'of', but their difference of form expresses a meaning distinction which is very important in Maori, a distinction which can best be expressed by the terms 'dominance' and 'subordination'. Possession of anything towards which the possessor is dominant, active or superior, is expressed by *a*; possession of things in respect to which the possessor is subordinate, passive or inferior, is expressed by *o*. *Te waiata a te tangata ra* 'that man's song' refers to a song which he composed or sang; *te waiata o te tangata ra* refers to a song which is about, or concerns the man. A person is active towards a book, in the sense that he can pick it up and carry it. Hence *te pukapuka a te tangata*. He is passive in respect of his canoe in the sense that it carries him. Hence *te waka o te tangata*. It is a fairly general rule that portable possessions are possessed by *a*, non-portables by *o*. But there are exceptions. Parts of things, including all articles of clothing, are possessed by *o*. Food, towards which one is obviously active, takes *a*. But drinking water takes *o*.

As we have seen above, the same noun may be possessed by *a* or *o* according to circumstance. The biblical book of Job, for example, is *Te Pukapuka o Hopa,* since it is about, not by him. On the other hand the Book of Daniel which is attributed to its central character is *Te Pukapuka a Raaniera.*

Nouns derived from verbal bases take *a* or *o* according to the situation being expressed. If the possessor is the actor in the sentence, possession will be marked by *a*; if the possessor is the goal of the sentence, possession will be marked by *o*. *Te patunga a Kupe i te wheke* 'Kupe's killing of the octopus', but *te patunga o te wheke* e *Kupe* 'the killing of the octopus by Kupe'. These sentences may be regarded as transforms respectively of the verbal sentences *ka patu a Kupe i te wheke* 'Kupe kills the octopus' and *ka patua te wheke* e *Kupe* 'the octopus is killed by Kupe'.

Nouns derived from stative bases always take *o*, for the meaning of a stative is always in a sense passive, never active. *Te matenga o te hoariri* 'the defeat of the enemy', never *te matenga a te hoariri*.

13.2 Summary of the uses of *a* and *o*

Use *a*:

(a) When the possessor is active or dominant or superior to that which is possessed. This includes the case when that which is possessed is a universal base (16.3) or a noun derived from an active universal base.

(b) When that which is possessed is portable.

(c) With food.

(d) With domestic animals (except horses), with children, with slaves or servants.

Use *o*:

(e) When the possessor is passive, subordinate or inferior to that which is possessed. This includes the case of a noun derived from (i) a stative base, or (ii) a universal base used passively.

(f) With means of transport, including horses.

(g) With drinking water.

(h) With parts, qualities, feelings, emotions, clothing, and *ingoa* 'name'.

(j) With relatives other than husband, wife, child, grandchild.

13.3 Pronunciation note

A and *o* are pronounced short before *te* and other syllables containing only one vowel; but they are pronounced long before syllables containing more than one vowel.

13.4 Examples

(Track 13 of the recordings.)

(a) *Te Waiata a Horomona.*
    Solomon's Song.

    Te patunga a Kupe i te wheke.
    Kupe's killing of the octopus.

    Nga mahi a nga tuupuna.
    The deeds of the ancestors.

    (b) *Te mere a te rangatira.*
        The chief's greenstone club.

        Te kete a te wahine.
        The woman's basket.

    (c) *Nga kuumara a Whakaotirangi.*
        Whakaotirangi's sweet potatoes.

        He koorero te kai a te rangatira.
        Talking is the food of chiefs.

    (d) *Nga tamariki a teeraa wahine.*
        That woman's children.

        Nga hipi a te kaimahi paamu.
        The farmer's sheep.

        Nga herehere a te taua.
        The prisoners of the war party.

    (e) (i) *Te rangatira o te iwi.*
            The chief of the tribe.

            Te matenga o te hoariri.
            The defeat of the enemy.

            Te rironga o te wahine.
            The abduction of the woman.

        (ii) *Te patunga o te wheke e Kupe.*
            The killing of the octopus by Kupe.

    (f) *Te waka o Hoturoa.*
        The canoe of Hoturoa.

        Te motokaa o Haamuera.
        Samuel's car.

    (g) *Te wai maaori o te puna ra.*
        The fresh water of that spring.

(h) *Te kakau o te toki.*
The handle of the axe.

Te aroha o te wahine.
The woman's love.

Te reka o te huka.
The sweetness of the sugar.

Te pootae o te kiingi.
The king's hat.

(j) *Te matua o te tamaiti.*
The child's parent.

Te tungaane o te kootiro.
The girl's brother.

Ko te wahine naana te waiata nei, aa, ko toona taane moona nei te waiata, eetahi o nga rangatira o Ngaati-Porou. Ko Turuhira Hine-i-whaakina te wahine rahi o oona hapuu, o Te Aitanga-a-Mate, o Te Whaanau-a-Raakairoa, o Te Ao-wera, o Te Whaanau-a-Ruataupare hoki ki Tuupaaroa. Teeraa anoo te taane i koorerotia maana, kaoore i pai atu, ka moe i a Te Manana Kaua-te-rangi.
The woman whose song this is, and her husband for whom the song (was sung) were high-ranking members of Ngaati-Porou tribe. Turuhira Hine-i-whaakina was the most prominent woman of her subtribes Te Aitanga-a-Mate, Te Whaanau-a-Raakairoa, Te Ao-wera, and Te Whaanau-a-Ruataupare at Tuupaa-roa. There was another husband bespoken for her, but (she) did not like him and she married Te Manana Kaua-te-rangi.

14. The possessive particles *ta* and *to*, and the T-class possessives

14.1 *Te a, te o*, and *ta, to*

Constructions such as *te waiata a Horomona* 'Solomon's song' and *te whakaaro o te wahine* 'the woman's thought' have transforms *ta Horomona waiata* and *to te wahine whakaaro.*

Let us consider what takes place when *te waiata a Horomona* is transformed to *ta Horomona waiata.* If we regard the possessive particle *ta* as being a combination of *te* 'definite article singular' plus *a* 'possessive particle of dominant possession' we can see that what was literally 'the song of Solomon' has become, as it were, 'the-of-Solomon song'. Similarly the possessive particle *to* is regarded as a combination of *te* and *o* 'possessive particle of subordinate possession', and *to te wahine whakaaro* is literally 'the-of-the-woman thought'.

Now observe what happens when that which is possessed is plural. *Nga waiata a Horomona* 'the songs of Solomon' has the transform *aa Horomona waiata*, and *nga whakaaro o te wahine* 'the thoughts of the woman' becomes *oo te wahine whakaaro.* In these examples the plural definite article *nga* is replaced by zero in the transform. The transform is parallel to the transform learned earlier (3.3) when *te whare nei* 'this house' became *teenei whare,* and *nga whare nei* 'these houses' became *eenei whare.*

The loss of an initial *t* to mark plural is a feature of *teenei, teenaa, teeraa, ta, to* and a number of other words which are called definitives. Definitives will be discussed as a group in 15.

14.2 The T-class possessives

The transforms with *ta* and *to* given above are characteristic of a rather formal style of speech. But the possessive particles *ta* and *to* enter into constructions with the personal pronouns to form a class of possessive pronouns which are extremely common, and basic to knowledge of Maori. These T-class possessives correspond to the English possessive adjectives 'my, your, his, their', etc. But unlike English, Maori marks the number of the item possessed, as well as the person and number of the possessor. Thus *ta raaua pukapuka* 'their book' but *aa raaua pukapuka* 'their books'.

The set of dual and plural T-class possessives follows:

	Dual	Plural
1st Person inclusive	*ta/to taaua*	*ta/to taatou*
1st Person exclusive	*ta/to maaua*	*ta/to maatou*
2nd Person	*ta/to koorua*	*ta/to koutou*
3rd Person	*ta/to raaua*	*ta/to raatou*

The singular forms are irregular. Instead of combining the singular personal pronouns with the possessive particles, these pronouns are replaced by three suffixes *-ku* 'first person singular', *-u* 'second person singular' and *-na* 'third person singular'. The possessives are now:

1st person singular *taaku, tooku*
2nd person singular *taau, toou*
3rd person singular *taana, toona*

There are in addition three 'neutral' forms which do not make the distinction between 'dominant' and 'subordinate' possession. They are *taku* 'first person singular', *to* 'second person singular', and *tana* 'third person singular'. Their use will be discussed in 15.4.

14.3 Examples

(These examples may be heard on Track 14 of the recordings.)

Tiikina taaku tamaiti.
Fetch my child.

Tiikina aaku tamariki.
Fetch my children.

Kua toto tooku ihu.
My nose has been bleeding.

14.3

Kua toto ooku taringa.
My ears have been bleeding.

Anei to maaua rangatira.
Here is our chief.

Anei oo maaua rangatira.
Here are our chiefs.

Kua tae mai aa taatou manuhiri.
Our guests have arrived.

E whaangai ana ia i taana kaawhe.
He is feeding his calf.

15. The definitives

15.1 The composition of the definitives

The list of definitives includes the singular and plural definite articles, and a number of composite items each of which comprises some form of the definite article plus (a) one of the positional particles *nei, na, ra* or (b) a possessive particle *a* or *o*, with or without a following personal pronoun or (c) the base *whea*. Examples are (a) *teenei* 'this', (b) *ta taatou* 'our' (c) *teewhea?* 'which one?'

Every definitive has a plural formed by deleting the initial *t* of the singular, thus *eenei* 'these', *aa taatou* 'our, plural', *eewhea?* 'which ones?'

Definitives normally occur in the preposed periphery of nominal phrases: *teenei tangata* 'this man'; *aa taatou tamariki* 'our children'; *teewhea tangata?* 'which man?'. Some definitives may also occur as the nuclei of phrases, e.g., *ko teenei* 'this one', *ko eeraa* 'those ones'.

15.2 Full inventory of definitives

Definite articles
  te, nga

possessive definitives
  ta, to

T-class possessives
  taaku, tooku, taku, taau, toou, to, taana, toona, tana, ta taaua, to taaua, ta maaua, to maaua, ta koorua, to koorua, ta raaua, to raaua, ta taatou, to taatou, ta maatou, to maatou, ta koutou, to koutou, ta raatou, to raatou

demonstratives
  teenei, teenaa, teeraa, taua

which?
  teewhea?

a certain
  teetahi

15.3 Examples

(Track 15 of the recordings.)

Kua mate tooku hoa.
My friend has died.

Kei hea ooku huu?
Where are my shoes?

He aha teenei?
What is this?

He aha eenei?
What are these?

Ta te rangatira kai he koorero.
Talk is the food of chiefs.

Kua moe wahine to koutou rangatira.
Your chief has taken a wife.

Teetahi rangatira no Te Wai-pounamu.
A certain chief from the South Island.

Ko Ahu te ingoa o taua whenua.
Ahu is the name of that (aforementioned) place.

15.4 The neutral T-class possessives *taku, to, tana*

The neutral T-class possessives *taku* 'my', *to* 'thy', and *tana* 'his, her' and their plural forms *aku, oo, ana* are used only in the preposed periphery of phrases, never in the nucleus position. They are used without regard to the *a* and *o* classes of possession. Thus *taku* may replace both *taaku* and *tooku*, *to* may replace both *taau* and *toou* and *tana* may replace both *taana* and *toona* in the preposed periphery of a phrase.

15.41 Examples

(Track 15 of the recordings)

Kua mate taku hoa.
My friend has died.

Kei hea aku huu?
Where are my shoes?

Tiikina taku tamaiti.
Fetch my child.

Tiikina aku tamariki.
Fetch my children.

Ka toto aku taringa.
My ears are bleeding.

E whaangai ana ia i tana kaawhe.
He is feeding his calf.

No hea to hoa, e Rewi?
Where does your friend come from Rewi?

Hei aha to oka, e Rewi?
What is your butcher-knife for, Rewi?

Kei hea taku koti, Maarama?
Where is my coat, Maarama?

Kei hea oo huu, e Riki?
Where are your shoes, Riki?

Haere koe ki te horoi i oo ringa!
Go and wash your hands!

I teetahi poo ka tae mai te waea ki a Hata kua mate tana mokopuna.
One night a telegram reached Heta (telling him that) his grandchild was
dead.

Ka kite atu a Tamahae i ana paraikete i runga kee i te moenga o Rewi.
Tamahae saw his blankets on Rewi's bed.

15.5 *Nei* after a T-class possessive or the retrospective definitive *taua*

Nei 'near speaker in space or time', usually a postposed particle, may be inserted after a T-class possessive, or *taua* 'the aforementioned' in the preposed periphery of a phrase. E.g. *Taua nei tangata* 'that person just mentioned', *ta taaua nei tamaiti* 'our child here'.

16. Parts of speech: the base classes

16.1 General

In 1.1 we examined the structure of the Maori phrase, which consists of a nucleus or central portion which contains one or more bases carrying the lexical meaning of the phrase. Peripheral to the nucleus are the preposed and postposed peripheral slots (positions), either or both of which may be filled by various particles which add the grammatical meaning of the phrase. *Whare* means 'house'. The addition of the preposed particle *te* gives *te whare* 'the house'. Adding the postposed particle *nei* 'here' gives *te whare nei* 'this house'.

Maanu means 'afloat'. The preposed verbal particle *i* 'past tense' gives *i maanu* 'was afloat'; adding the postposed particle *anoo* 'again' gives *i maanu anoo* 'was afloat again'.

Those words which can fill the nucleus slot of the phrases are called bases. The words which precede and follow the nucleus in the peripheral slots of the phrases are called particles. All bases contain at least one stressed syllable. Particles are unstressed.

It turns out that not all particles can occur with all bases. Some bases, for example, take the definite article *te* before them in some phrases. Others never do so. Many bases take verbal particles, others never do. Even where two bases can both occur with the same particle, the position in which the particle occurs with respect to the base may differ. Both *runga* 'top' and *raatou* 'they' are compatible with the preposed particle *ki* 'to'. But *ki* precedes *runga* directly as in *ki runga* 'to the top', while the proper article *a* must always occur between *ki* and *raatou* as in *ki a raatou* 'to them'.

If different bases combine in different ways with particles it is clear that some method of classifying the bases must be found. It is in this respect that all traditional grammars of Maori fail, for although they talk about different parts of speech it is never made clear how to decide what part of speech a given word is. The relevant section in the Introduction to Williams's Maori Dictionary, for example, says 'most words may be used in more than one of the classes of parts of speech.' But we need to know *what* words (bases) may be used in *what* classes of parts of speech, and before this can be stated we have to know what the parts of speech are.

In Williams's Maori Dictionary and in *First Lessons in Maori* by the same author we find listed all of the parts of speech familiar to us from English grammar, plus three others: the definitives, local nouns, and neuter verbs.

Unfortunately, as we have been warned, a word may occur in several of the 'classes of parts of speech'. The word *pai* 'good', for example, is listed in Williams's Dictionary as being an adjective, noun, neuter verb and transitive verb. On the other hand *raakau* 'wood' is listed only as a noun. *Tangi* 'weep' is listed as a verb and a noun; *tika* 'straight, correct' only as an adjective; *tapu* 'sacred, prohibited' as adjective and noun.

It is clear that, in the traditional view of Maori grammar, there are a large number of parts of speech (at least eight), and a given word may, at different times, be any one of several parts of speech. But this, in effect, greatly increases the number of parts of speech since *raakau* is a noun, *tangi* a verb-noun, *pai* an adjective-noun-neuter-verb and transitive verb, and so on. And there is *no way of knowing how many parts of speech a given word embraces* without consulting all of its definitions in the dictionary.

In *Let's Learn Maori* an entirely different grammatical theory is used and a much simplified system of classification results. All words are divided into two classes, bases and particles. The particles (and certain affixes) are the grammatical words; they are few in number, and each must be discussed in detail as the course progresses.

All other words are bases. Bases divide into five classes (parts of speech). The class of a base is determined by the constructions into which it can enter. *There are no overlapping classes.* A noun can never be a stative; a locative can never be a universal. The classification of a base as a noun, a stative, a universal, a locative, or a personal, tells us all that needs to be known about the grammatical constructions into which it can enter.

Before discussing each of the five base classes in detail it would be well to remind ourselves that phrases, the most important structural units of Maori, are divided into two classes: verbal phrases (marked as such by a verbal particle), and nominal phrases (all others).

16.2 Nouns

Some bases, of which *ika* 'fish', *kiore* 'rat' and *raakau* 'tree' are examples, occur as the nucleus of nominal phrases, but not in verbal phrases. They are nouns. (Before saying, 'Of course "fish, rat, tree" are nouns', remember that two of the English words, at least, can be used as verbs.) In saying that a Maori word is a noun class base, we are saying that it *never* occurs in a verbal use. It is like the English word 'door' or 'song', not like 'fish' or 'tree' both of which can be used in verbal as well as nominal constructions. The nouns *ika, kiore,* and *raakau* occur in such phrases as *te ika, nga raakau, he kiore,* but never in such phrases as **e ika ana, *ka raakau,* or **kua kiore.*

> A noun is any word which can take a definite article but which cannot occur as the nucleus of a verbal phrase

16.3 Universals

Some bases, of which *inu* 'drink', *tangi* 'weep' and *kii* 'say' are examples, can be used passively (7). Any such base is a universal. Universals have a very wide distribution, being able to enter into nominal as well as verbal phrases. It is probable that universals form the largest class of Maori words. The three quoted are shown to be universals by such phrases as *e inumia ana* 'is being drunk', *e tangihia ana* 'is being wept for', *kua kiia* 'has been said'.

> A universal is any word which may be used passively

16.4 Statives

Some bases, of which *ora* 'well', *tika* 'correct' and *maanu* 'afloat' are examples, occur in verbal phrases, but are never used passively (i.e. with passive suffixes). Such words are statives. Most statives can also occur in non-verbal phrases, but a few of them, *maanu* 'afloat' is one, are seldom if ever used other than verbally. Note in the following examples that statives are best translated by English adjectives or participles.

16.4

Kia ora koutou!
Greetings! (literally 'may you be well').

He maha nga toa i mate i a ia i taua waa.
Many warriors were defeated by him at that time.

Ka wera te whare i te ahi.
The house was destroyed by fire.

Ka tika taau koorero.
Your talk is correct.

> A stative is any base which can be used verbally but
> not passively

16.41 Stative Verbs

While most statives can occur as the head of both verbal and nominal phrases, there is a small subclass which can occur only in verbal phrases. Members of this subclass (which are distinguished as Sv in the vocabulary in this book) are:

pau 'all used up, exhausted'
mutu 'ended, finished'
oti 'completed, finished'
ngaro 'out of sight, lost'
mahue 'abandoned, left behind'
mau 'held fast, caught'
riro 'gone, taken'
ea 'requited, avenged, paid'
tuu 'wounded'
whara 'injured, struck'
maakona 'satisfied (of appetite), replete'
maanu 'afloat'.

Ka maanu ia i te au o te moana.
He floated on the current of the sea.

Kua Mutu te mahi.
The work is ended.

Kua oti te mahi.
The work is completed.

Kei whara koe!
Don't get hurt (be careful!).

Kaahore anoo kia ea tana mate.
His death has not been avenged yet.

16.5 Locatives

Some bases never occur in verbal phrases, and never take any form of the definite article. They can be preceded directly by the locative particles *ki, i, kei.* Such bases are called locatives. Locatives were discussed in 12. Note that all place names are locatives.

> A locative is any base which can follow the locative
> particle *ki* directly

16.6 Personals

Personals include all personal names, and names of things which have been personified, e.g. a meeting-house which bears the name of an ancestor. The names of the months are personals. The personal pronouns are a special subclass of personals which differ slightly from other personals in the way they are used (see 9.1). The interrogative *wai* 'who?' and *Mea* 'So-and-so' are personals.

> A personal is any base which requires the personal
> article *a* after the locative particle *ki*

17. Prepositions

17.1 General

The preposed particles *ko, me, ma, mo, na, no, ki, i, kei, hei, a, o,* most of which have already been mentioned, share a number of features in common.

(i)   They all occur only as the first word in a phrase.
(ii) They are all mutually incompatible (i.e. no two of them may occur in the same phrase).
(iii) They all indicate a particular relationship between the phrase in which they occur and the rest of the sentence.
(iv) They never occur in verbal phrases.
(v)   They all occur with the same base classes, and, with an exception to be discussed below, in the same position respective to them.

Since these particles have so much in common we will find it convenient to refer to them collectively as prepositions. The similarity of their grammatical relations allows us to discuss them together.

17.2 The paradigm of prepositions

me   conjunctive, 'and, with'
ko   focus
a   dominant possession, 'of'
o   subordinate possession, 'of'
ma   unrealised dominant possession, 'for'
mo   unrealised subordinate possession, 'for'
na   realised dominant possession, 'of, by'
no   realised subordinate possession, 'of'
ki   motion towards, 'to'
i   past position, 'at'
kei present position, 'at'
hei future position, 'at'

17.3 The structure of prepositional phrases

Any phrase beginning with a preposition is a prepositional phrase.

17.31 Prepositional phrases containing nouns, statives and universals
If the prepositional phrase contains a noun, stative or universal as nucleus a definitive (15) will occur between the preposition and the nucleus.

PREPOSITION	DEFINITIVE	NOUN STATIVE UNIVERSAL

Ki tooku kaainga (N) 'to my home'; *ko te rangatira* (S) 'the chief'; *o aaku mahi* (U) 'of my deeds'.

17.32 Prepositional phrases containing locatives
If the prepositional phrase contains a locative as nucleus no other particle will occur between the preposition and the nucleus.

PREPOSITION	LOCATIVE

Kei runga 'on top'; *ki runga* 'to the top'; *o runga* 'of the top'; *mo runga* 'for the top'; *ko runga* 'the top'; *hei runga* 'to be on top'.

17.33 Prepositional phrases with *ki, i, kei, hei* and a personal
If the prepositional phrase begins with *ki, i, kei, hei,* and contains a personal as nucleus, the personal will be preceded by the personal article *a*.

ki *i* *kei* *hei*	*a*	PERSONAL

17.33

Ki a raatou 'to them'; *kei a maatou* 'with (at) us'; *i a wai?* 'with whom ? (past)'; *hei a Tiihema* 'in December (future)'.

17.34 Other prepositional phrases and personals

If the prepositional phrase begins with any preposition other than *ki, i, kei, hei,* and contains a personal as nucleus, the preposition will immediately precede the personal.

me *ko* *ma* *mo* *na* *no* *a* *o*	PERSONAL

Ma Pita 'for Peter'; *ko Maarama* 'Maarama'; *no wai?* 'belonging to whom?'; *a maatou* 'of us'.

18. The possessive prepositions *na, no, ma, mo*

(Examples from this section may be heard on Track 16 of the recordings.)

18.1 Pronunciation note

Before a short syllable (i.e. a syllable containing only one vowel) *na, no, ma, mo* are pronounced short; before a syllable containing more than one vowel they are pronounced long.

18.2 *Na* and *no*

Basically *na* and *no* have the meaning 'belonging to, of' with the special implication that the possession is already an accomplished fact. The difference between *na* and *no* is the usual distinction between 'dominant' and 'subordinate' possession (13).

Na wai te mea nei?
Who owns this thing?

Na Pita.
Peter does.

No te iwi katoa nga whenua.
The lands belong to the whole tribe.

Na te rangatira teenei tamaiti.
This child is the chief's.

No nga kootiro eeraa piupiu.
Those dance-skirts belong to the girls.

18.21 *Na* and *no* with locatives

When used with a locative *na* means 'by way of'. *Na hea mai koutou?* 'By way of what place did you come?'

18.21

No with Locatives has the meaning 'from'. *No hea koe? No Aakarana ahau.*
'Where are you from? I am from Auckland.'

18.22 *Na reira, no reira*

Na reira and *no reira* both mean 'therefore'. The usual distinction between *na* and *no* does not seem to apply here. Some dialect areas tend to use *na reira* exclusively, while speakers from other areas use *no reira*.

18.3 *Ma* and *mo*

Basically *ma* and *mo* have the meaning of 'possession not yet realised'. 'For' is often a good translation.

Ma Pita teenei pukapaka.
This book is for Peter.

Mo wai teeraa whare?
Who is that house for?

Mo nga manuhiri tuaarangi.
For the visitors from afar.

18.31 *Mo* may mean 'concerning'

Mo may often be translated appropriately by 'concerning, about' as in *he waiata teenei mo Paapaka* 'this is a song concerning Paapaka', *he koorero teenei mo Hine-koorangi* 'this is a story about Hine-koorangi'.

18.32 *Ma* with a locative means 'by way of'

Ma hea mai koutou?
What way did you come?

Ma runga i te waka o Pani.
By Pani's canoe.

Ma runga o te maunga.
By way of the mountain top.

Ma hea mai to koutou ara?
By way of what route did you come?

I haere mai maatou ma te maania o Kaingaroa, ma te ara ki Waiotapu.
We came by way of Kaingaroa Plains, by the road to Waiotapu.

18.4 N-class and M-class possessive pronouns

Both *na, no* and *ma, mo* combine with the personal pronouns to form possessive pronouns. As with the T-class possessive pronouns (14.2) the singular forms are irregular.

	SINGULAR	DUAL	PLURAL
1ST PERSON INCL.		*na/no taaua*	*na/no taatou*
		ma/mo taaua	*ma/mo taatou*
1ST PERSON EXCL.	*naaku, nooku*	*na/no maaua*	*na/no maatou*
	maaku, mooku	*ma/mo maaua*	*ma/mo maatou*
2ND PERSON	*naau, noou*	*na/no koorua*	*na/no koutou*
	maau, moou	*ma/mo koorua*	*ma/mo koutou*
3RD PERSON	*naana, noona*	*na/no raaua*	*na/no raatou*
	maana, moona	*ma/mo raaua*	*ma/mo raatou*

18.5 Examples

I tiikina atu he wai mo raatou.
Water was fetched for them.

Mo koutou teenei whare.
This house is for you.

18.5

Naaku teenaa naihi.
That knife is mine.

Na wai maa, nga kai nei?
Who owns this food?

Na nga tamariki o te kura.
The school children.

Na wai te kurii ra?
Whose dog is that?

Na te wahine a Mookena.
It belongs to Mookena's wife.

He tuahine a Horowai no Hoani.
Horowai is a sister of John's.

He tuakana koe nooku.
You are a senior relative of mine.

Na raatou nga hipi nei.
These sheep belong to them.

Moona te wai.
The water is for him.

19. The imperative with universals

(Examples from this section may be heard on Track 17 of the recording.)

19.1 General

There are a number of ways of expressing an imperative (giving an order) in Maori. They are all marked by an imperative intonation as can be readily heard on the recording.

19.2 Active universals with imperative intonation

Any universal base may be used with imperative intonation to give an order. Imperative intonation is marked in writing by an exclamation mark (!). If the universal contains no more than two vowels (and if there are no postposed particles other than *ra)*, the verbal particle *e* will be preposed, thus:

E tuu!	stand!
e noho!	sit!
e ara!	get up!
e moe!	go to sleep!
e oho!	wake up!
e kai!	eat!
e noho ra!	goodbye!
e moe ra!	go to sleep!

If the base (or the phrase) contains more than two vowels the preposed *e* will not be used:

maranga!	arise!
takoto!	lie down!
tomo mai!	come in!
karanga atu!	call!
haere mai!	come here (welcome)!
haere atu!	go away!

whakarongo!	listen!
titiro mai!	look here!
haere koe!	you go!

19.3 Passive imperatives

The imperatives in the preceding section imply no goal (object) of the action which is ordered. Where an object or goal is implied or expressed the construction known as the passive imperative is used. This is simply the passive form of the universal base, with imperative intonation, but without preposed verbal particle. The goal may be expressed, or implied:

nohoia!	sit on (it)!
moea!	marry (her)!
karangatia atu!	call (him)!
tirohia!	look at (it)!
kainga!	eat (it)!
patua te kurii ra!	kill that dog!
kimihia te mea ngaro!	seek that which is lost!
whaaia te maatauranga!	seek knowledge!
murua oo maatou hara!	forgive us our sins!
kapia te kuuwaha!	shut the door!
whakapuaretia te mataaho!	open the window!
tapahia te paraaoa!	cut the bread!
tiikina atu he wai mooku!	fetch me some water!
tiikina he ahi i a Mahuika!	fetch some fire from Mahuika!
haria he kai ma taaua!	bring some food for us!
hopukia! patua kia mate!	seize (him)! kill him!

Tukua atu te Kaawana kia hoki ki toona kaainga!
Let the Governor go back to his own place!

19.4 Actions of body-parts

An order to perform an action with any part of the body involves a special construction using the body-part as if it were the actor in the sentence. Thus:

haamama toou waha!
open your mouth! [not **haamama i toou waha!* – the fact that the nominal phrase is not initiated by one of the comment marking particles *i* or *ki* (6) makes it appear that Maori regards the body-part itself as being the actor in such constructions]

Totoro mai toou ringa!
Hold out your hand!

Titiro oou kanohi!
Open your eyes!

Piko toou maatenga!
Bow your head!

Tahuri mai toou tinana!
Turn your body this way!

Takahi toou wae!
Stamp your foot!

19.5 Weak imperatives with *me*

Any universal may be preposed by the verbal particle *me* to indicate a weak imperative. Syntactically the verbal phrase may be either active or passive, but the base will not take a passive suffix. The verbal particle *me* and the passive suffix are incompatible:

Me haere taatou!	Let's go!
Mc karanga ahau!	I had better call!
Me kawe koe i taku kete!	You must carry my kit!
Me kawe e koe taku kete!	My kit must be carried by you!

19.6 Examples

Ka kii atu a Kupe, 'Purutia iho to wheke! E haere ana nga waka aapoopoo ki te hii ika.'
Kupe said, 'Restrain your octopus! The canoes are going fishing tomorrow.'

Ka hoki a Kupe ki te iwi, ka mea atu, 'Mahia taku waka kia pai!'
Kupe returned to the tribe and said, 'Prepare my canoe!'

Ka kii atu a Kupe ki tana wahine, 'Hoake ki runga i te waka kia kotahi ai to taaua mate!'
Kupe said to his wife, 'Go onto the canoe so that we two shall die together!'

Ka karanga a Kupe, 'Makaia nga tahaa na ki te upoko o te wheke!'
Kupe called, 'Throw these calabashes onto the head of the octopus!'

20. Negative transforms of verbal sentences

(Examples from this section may be heard on Track 18 of the recordings.)

20.1 General

It is possible, and indeed usual, to regard a negative sentence as the 'transform' of a corresponding affirmative sentence. In the examples that follow notice that in every case the negative transform of an affirmative sentence involves the use of both a 'negative formula' and an alteration of phrase order. The negative formula consists of a negative word, or phrase, which is paired with a particular verbal particle. Thus the negative transform of an affirmative sentence in the past tense is formed with *kiihai* paired with the verbal particle *i* (20.3). To take another example, the negative phrase *kaahore anoo* is paired with the verbal particle *kia* as the negative formula used to transform an affirmative sentence in the perfect tense with *kua* (20.4).

20.2 *Kaahore . . . e . . . ana*: the continuous tense, affirmative and negative

> *E koorero ana nga waahine.*
> The women are talking.

> *Kaahore nga wahine e koorero ana.*
> The women are not talking.

Notice that in this affirmative active sentence the verbal phrase is followed by the actor phrase, but the negative sentence begins with the negative formula, which is then followed by the actor and action, in inverted order.

> *E aawhinatia ana nga waahine.*
> The women are being helped.

> *Kaahore nga waahine e aawhinatia ana.*
> The women are not being helped.

Notice that in the case of this passive affirmative sentence and its negative transform the same changes are involved, namely the introduction of the sentence by the negative formula, and the inversion of order of the verbal phrase, and, in this case, its goal.

E tika ana te koorero.
The talk is correct.

Kaahore te koorero e tika ana.
The talk is not correct.

Once again, this time in a stative sentence, the negative transform involves the use of the negative formula and an inversion of order.

20.3 *Kiihai . . . i*: the past tense, affirmative and negative

I haere maatou.
We went.

Kiihai maatou i haere.
We did not go.

I whakautua taaku reta.
My letter was answered.

Kiihai taaku reta i whakautua.
My letter was not answered.

I hinga te raakau.
The tree fell.

Kiihai te raakau i hinga.
The tree did not fall.

The negative transforms of past tense sentences are formed by the negative formula *kiihai . . . i* and the usual inversion of predicate and subject.

20.4 *Kaahore anoo . . . kia*: the perfect tense, affirmative and negative

Kua haere atu te tangata ra.
That man has gone away.

Kaahore anoo te tangata ra kia haere atu.
That man has not gone away.

Kua karangatia nga tamariki.
The children have been called.

Kaahore anoo nga tamariki kia karangatia.
The children have not been called (yet).

Kua mate te wahine.
The woman has died.

Kaahore anoo te wahine kia mate.
The woman has not died (yet).

Notice that in the negative transform of affirmative perfect tense sentences the verbal particle *kua* is replaced by *kia*. *Kaahore* is usually, but not obligatorily, followed by *anoo* in this construction. The usual inversion of order applies.

20.5 *E kore . . . e*: the future tense, affirmative and negative

E haere koe aapoopoo.
You will go tomorrow.

E kore koe e haere aapoopoo.
You will not go tomorrow.

The negative formula is *e kore . . . e* and the usual inversion of order applies. It should be noted that in modern Maori the affirmative future tense is seldom used. Its place is almost always taken by the inceptive tense with *ka* (20.6).

20.6 The inceptive tense with *ka*

A sentence in the inceptive tense, with *ka*, has no formal negative transform. If the real time of the action is in the past *kiihai . . . i* will provide an appropriate negative; if the time is future a negative with *e kore . . . e* is appropriate.

20.7 *Kaua . . . e*: the negative imperative with universals

Haere!
Go!

Kaua e haere!
Do not go!

E noho!
Sit!

Kaua e noho!
Don't sit!

Patua!
Kill (it)!

Kaua e patua!
Don't kill (it)!

Notice that only universals occur in this construction. Where the subject is expressed there will be the usual inversion of order.

Kaua koutou e haina i teenaa pepa!
Don't sign that paper!

Haere taatou!
Let's go!

Kaua taatou e haere!
Let's not go!

Kaua ahau e whakareerea!
Let me not be cast aside!

Kaua teenei taura e puritia!
Don't hang on to this rope!

Ka kii atu a Kupe, 'Purutia iho to wheke! Kaua e tukua atu ki te moana!'
Kupe said, 'Restrain your octopus! Don't let it go out on the sea!'

Ka kii te hunaonga ki toona hungawai, 'Ki te tohe koe kia riro to kootiro i a koe ka mate koe. Kaua e tohe mai!'
The son-in-law said to the father-in-law, 'If you persist in taking your daughter with you, you will die. Don't argue!'

20.8 Negative imperative in subordinate clauses

In subordinate clauses the negative imperative *kaua . . . e* is preceded by *kia.* Study the following examples:

Ka mea mai te ariki kia kaua raatou e haere ki reira.
The high chief said that they should not go to that place.

I mea mai a Kupe ki a au kia kaua e kawea keetia te ihu o te waka i te putanga mai o te raa.
Kupe said to me that the bow of the canoe should not be diverted from the place where the sun rises.

21. The directional particles *mai, atu, iho, ake*

(The examples in this section may be heard on Track 19 of the recordings.)

21.1 General

Mai 'towards speaker', *atu* 'away from speaker', *iho* 'downwards', and *ake* 'upwards' are postposed particles, typically, and very frequently, found in verbal phrases. It is a striking feature of Maori that most actions are given a directional aspect by the use of one of these particles, often when the idea of actual movement does not seem at all appropriate to the verb expressed.

21.2 *Mai*

Mai has the basic meaning of 'hither, towards speaker' as in the favourite Maori phrase of welcome *haere mai!* Similarly we have *tomo mai!* 'come in!', *titiro mai!* 'look here!', and *haria mai!* 'bring (it) here!' In these examples the idea of direction of action seems natural enough. In some of the examples which follow it may not seem so appropriate:

Kua tae mai nga manuwhiri.
The guests have arrived.

I kau mai te wahine nei i nga ahiahi katoa.
This woman swam hither every evening.

Ka tae mai ki a ia te hiahia kia kite i oona tunakana.
The desire to see his older brothers came to him.

Ka taaria nei a Rona e aana tamariki kia hoki mai ki te kaainga.
Rona's children waited for her to come back home.

E kiia mai ana, 'No hea teenei wahine?'
It is being said, 'Where does this woman come from?'

Titiro ki te maunga e tuu mai ana.
Look at the mountain standing there.

21.3 *Atu*

Atu has the basic meaning of 'direction away from speaker'. As with *mai* actual movement is not necessarily involved.

Hoki atu ki toou kaainga!
Go away home!

I haere mai nga maatua; ko nga tamariki i noho atu i te kaainga.
The parents came; the children remained at home.

Ka kite a Hinemoa i a Tuu-taanekai; ka titiro atu, ka titiro mai.
Hinemoa saw Tuu-taanekai; (she) looked (at him), (he) looked (at her).

21.31 *Atu* with *kawe* and *tiki*
With certain words such as *kawe* 'carry' and *tiki* 'fetch', *atu* is used where *mai* might be expected. The emphasis seems to be on the going to get something, rather than the bringing it back.

Kawea atu he wai mooku.
Carry (get) some water for me.

Haere ki te kaainga ki te tiki atu i te toki.
Go home and fetch the axe.

Tiikina atu te tiikera!
Fetch the kettle!

21.32 *Atu* as a comparative
In appropriate contexts *atu* translates the comparative degree of English adjectives, as in the following examples:

Pai atu teenei i teenaa.
This is better than that.

Nui atu te hiahia o Takarangi ki a Raumahora i te hiahia ki te riri.
Takarangi's love for Raumahora is greater than his love of war.

21.33 *Teetahi atu* and *teeraa atu*

The idioms *teetahi atu* and *teeraa atu* mean 'other, another' as in the following examples:

Hoomai teetahi atu!
Give me another!

Eeraa waka atu.
Those other canoes.

Te puuhaa, te waata kiriihi, me eeraa atu kai a te Maaori.
Puha, water-cress and other Maori foods.

21.34 *Hoatu, whoatu*

Hoatu and its dialectal variant *whoatu,* both written as one word, mean 'give away' or 'set out, go'.

Ka tae te tangata ra ki tana taurekareka, ka hoatu hei utu mo te wahine.
The man took his slave and gave him away as payment for the woman.

Hoatu! Me waiho maaua i konei!
Go on! Leave us here!

21.4 *Ake*

Ake has the basic meaning 'upwards' though this meaning is not always obvious:

Ka piki ake a Taawhaki ki te rangi.
Taawhaki climbed up to the sky.

Ka ora ake a Taawhaki i toona mate.
Taawhaki recovered from his illness.

I huu ake te puna i raro i te whenua.
The spring bubbled up from the ground.

Ka tuu ake au ki te koorero atu ki a koutou.
I stand up to speak to you.

Ka whakatika ake a Hinemoa i roto i te wai.
Hinemoa arose out of the water.

21.41 *Ake* as a comparative

In appropriate contexts *ake* may translate the comparative degree of English adjectives:

> *Kua haere ia ki runga ake.*
> He has gone higher up.

> *Pai ake teenei!*
> This is better.

21.42 *Ake* indicates immediate sequence in time

Ake may indicate immediate sequence in time:

> *i mua tata ake*
> shortly before

> *mea ake*
> presently

> *mea kau ake*
> immediately

> *ao ake te raa*
> next day

> *taro ake*
> shortly afterwards

> *i mua ake*
> a short time before

> *taua raa ake*
> that very day

21.43 *Ake* as a reflexive

English reflexive pronouns are translated by Maori pronouns followed by *ake* (or *anoo*, 41):

> *tooku whare ake* or *tooku ake whare*
> my own house

21.43

ki a raaua ake
to themselves

ana tama ake
his own sons

21.44 *Hoake*

Hoake is a compound of a bound root *ho-* plus *ake*. It means 'to set out, go' as in *hoake taatou ki te whare!* 'Let's go to the house'.

21.5 *Iho*

Iho means 'downwards'. When two things are one above the other, actually or figuratively, *iho* qualifies the action or condition of that which is in the superior position, while *ake* is used of that in the inferior position. When Whakatuuria was taken prisoner and hung up in a kit under the ridgepole of his captors' house the following conversation took place:

> *Ka mea ake raatou o te whare, 'E koe e iri iho nei, koorero iho ra!' Ka mea iho taua maaia ra, 'Te kino hoki o ta koutou haka e rongo iho nei au!' Ka mea ake taua iwi nei, 'He iwi pai koutou ki te haka?' Ka mea iho ia, 'Nui atu te pai!' Ka mea a Uenaku, 'Tukua iho!' Aa, tukua iho ana. Ka mea atu taua tangata, 'E haka!'*
> The people of the house said, 'You hanging up there, speak!' That fellow said, 'What a terrible *haka* it is that I can hear.' Those people said, 'Are your people good at *haka?*' He replied, 'Very good!' Uenuku then said, 'Let him down!' And he was released. That man then said, 'Dance!'

> *Ka tae a Maaui ki te rua i rere iho ra toona whaea.*
> Maaui reached the pit down which his mother had fled.

21.51 *Iho* and *ake* with going and staying

A person going away is regarded as being in the superior position with respect to those staying behind:

Hoki ana ia ki to raatou kaainga, i mea iho ia ki oona tuaakana, 'Haere ake i muri nei! Kia hohoro ake te haere!'
When he was returning home he said to his elder brothers, 'Come after me, and hurry!'

21.52 *Muri iho*

Iho is used with *muri* 'after, behind' to indicate immediate sequence in time.

I muri iho
soon afterwards

21.53 *Iho* as a comparative

In appropriate contexts *iho* may translate the comparative degree of an adjective.

Raro iho
lower, further down

iti iho
less, fewer

21.6 Examples

I a ia e haere atu ana, ka kitea mai e oona tuaakana.
As he was going he was seen by his older brothers.

Noho atu ana teetahi, noho mai ana teetahi, i teetahi taha, i teetahi taha, o taa raaua ahi.
They sat opposite one another on either side of their fire.

He aha koe i haere mai i te rourou iti a Haere, tee noho atu, i te tookanga nui a Noho?
Why did you come here for the short supplies of the traveller, and not remain at home with the plentiful provisions of the stay-at-home?

Ka uia mai e Tama, 'No hea teenei kai?' Ka karanga atu a Taukata, 'No Hawaiki!'
Tama asked, 'Where is this food from?' Taukata replied, 'From Hawaiki!'

22. The manner particles *rawa, tonu, kee, noa, pea, koa*

(Examples in this section may be heard on Track 20 of the recordings.)

22.1 General

The manner particles are a set of postposed particles, each of which qualifies the meaning of the phrase nucleus with some such meaning as is expressed in English by words like 'very, quite, still, perhaps, on the other hand, indeed'. In no case, however, is there an exact overlap between the meaning of an English word and the meaning of any one of the manner particles, a fact which makes their correct use difficult for English speakers.

22.2 *Rawa*

Rawa intensifies the meaning of the base in the phrase nucleus. It is often translated appropriately by 'very' or 'really'.

> *He pukapuka pai teenei? Aae, he pukapaka pai rawa.*
> Is this a good book? Yes, it is a very good book.

> *Kua kore te kai? Aae, kua kore rawa.*
> Is there no food. No, there's absolutely none.

> *He peewhea te kai nei? He pai rawa.*
> How is this food? Very good.

> *Ko te hiahia o Kupe, kia tae rawa atu ia ki Aotearoa.*
> It was Kupe's wish to get right to New Zealand.

> *I whara te tangata, kaahore i mate rawa.*
> The man was injured but not killed.

> *Kotahi te wahine pai rawa o teenei ope.*
> There is one really beautiful woman in this group.

22.3 *Tonu*

Tonu has the basic meaning of 'continuity'.

> *E haere tonu atu ana te tangata.*
> The man is continuing to move away.

> *He tangi tonu te mahi a te tamaiti nei.*
> This child is always crying.

> *E kore tonu au e whakaae.*
> I will never agree.

22.31 *Tonu* as an intensifier

> *Ko koe tonu!*
> You, yourself!

> *Poto tonu nga kai!*
> The food is all gone!

22.32 *Tonu atu* and *tonu mai* may indicate immediacy

Tonu sometimes indicates 'immediacy', especially when combined with *atu* or *mai*.

> *Tae tonu atu ia, ka moe.*
> As soon as he arrived he slept.

22.4 *Kee*

Kee indicates 'otherness, difference, unexpectedness'.

> *Kei hea kee nga tamariki ?*
> Where are the children ? (They are not where I expected them to be.)

> *Kua haere kee nga tamariki.*
> The children have gone (to another place).

22.4

E aha kee ana koutou?
What (on earth) are you doing?

I te aha kee koe inanahi?
What *were* you doing yesterday?

Kei Taranaki kee raatou e noho ana.
They are living away in Taranaki.

Kiihai te ika i mau ki te waha, i mau kee ki te hiku.
The fish was not caught by the mouth, it was foul-hooked by the tail.

Haere kee koe, haere kee ia.
You went one way, he went the other.

Me tango kee koe i teenei.
Take this one (not the other).

Kaua koe e huri kee!
Don't turn away!

22.5 *Noa*

Noa means 'without restriction or restraint, freely, without any set purpose, spontaneously, in vain'.

I haere noa maatou.
We just went (without any special reason).

I tukua te tangata kia haere noa.
The man was allowed to go free.

I makere noa iho te hua o te raakau.
The fruit just fell down.

Ehara eenei waahine i konei; no tawhiti noa atu raatou.
These women are not from here, but from a far distant place.

I karanga noa atu au ki a ia.
I called him in vain.

22.6 *Pea*

Pea means 'perhaps'.

Aae pea!
Yes, perhaps.

E kore pea ia e pai mai ki ahau.
Perhaps he won't like me.

22.7 *Koa*

Koa is a manner particle which is used with imperatives in the Waikato and North Auckland areas to translate English 'please'. *Hoomai koa te pata* 'please pass the butter'. It also occurs in a number of idioms where it adds emphasis or intensity. *Aha koa* (often written *ahakoa)* 'although', *teenaa koa!* 'let's see!'

Kiihai koa i taro, ka puta atu te tangata.
Indeed it was not long before the man appeared.

Ko koe anoo koa a Whakatau.
You are indeed Whakatau.

23. The verbal phrase

(Examples from this section may be heard on Track 21 of the recordings.)

23.1 Verbal phrases with preposed verbal particles

All that we have learned so far about verbal phrases can be summed up in the following formula where + indicates that the slot must be filled and ± indicates that it may or may not be filled.

± VERBAL PARTICLE (or imperative intonation) + NUCLEUS ± MANNER PARTICLE ± DIRECTIONAL PARTICLE ± POSITIONAL PARTICLE

Examine the following examples and note that in each case the verbal phrase conforms to the above formula:

Kua tae mai raatou.
They have arrived.

Kua tae mai nei raatou.
They have arrived here.

Kua tae tonu mai nei raatou.
They have just arrived here.

I haehae rawa raatou.
They slashed deeply.

I haehae rawa iho raatou.
They slashed deeply downwards.

I haehae rawa iho nei raatou.
They slashed deeply downwards here.

Kua haere atu ia.
He has gone away.

Kua haere kee atu ia.
He has already gone away.

Kua haere kee atu ra ia.
He has already gone away there.

It can be seen from the above examples that various possibilities of combination are possible in the postposed periphery of the verbal phrase. It is extremely important to notice, however, that the *order* of particles is rigidly fixed. First comes the manner particle (if any), then the directional particle (if any), and then the positional particle (if any).

23.2 Verbal phrases without preposed verbal particles

There are three different situations in which a verbal phrase may lack the usual preposed verbal particle, and in each case the phrase is still unambiguously marked as verbal.

23.21 Bases containing more than two vowels used imperatively

If a universal containing two vowels is used imperatively it will be preceded by the verbal particle *e,* and an imperative intonation will be used.

E tuu! 'stand!', *e noho!* 'sit!', *e kai!* 'eat!'

If, however, the base contains more than two vowels, or if there is anything (except *ra*) in the postposed periphery of the phrase, the verbal particle will be omitted. But the verbal status of the phrase will still be marked unambiguously by the imperative intonation.

Haere! 'go!', *takoto!* 'lie down!', *whakarongo mai!* 'listen!', *neke atu!* 'move over!'.

23.22 Phrases containing *ana* in the postposed periphery

Any phrase containing *ana* in the postposed periphery and nothing in the preposed periphery is classed as a verbal phrase. This usage is common in animated narrative in the past tense.

Noho ana ia, tunu manu ana maana.
He sat down and roasted birds for himself.

Kau atu ana raatou ki uta.
They swam away to shore.

23.23 Phrases containing *ai* in the postposed periphery

A phrase containing *ai* in the postposed periphery is marked as verbal even though there may be no verbal particle present. Such a phrase usually forms a subordinate constituent of the sentence indicating an action or state which is consequent upon some earlier circumstance.

Haere mai ki konei, noho ai.
Come here and sit down.

Kei konei pea taaua mate ai.
Here perhaps, we two shall die.

24. The actor emphatic

(Examples from this section may be heard on Track 22 of the recordings.)

24.1 General

When it is necessary to emphasise the actor in a verbal sentence it may be placed at the beginning of the sentence (in focus position; see 38.3), introduced by the focus particle *ko*. Or the actor may be introduced by one of the possessive particles *na, no,* or *ma* as in the construction to be described below, and called the actor emphatic.

24.2 Future actor emphatic with *ma . . . e*

The particle *ma,* or one of the M-class possessives derived from it (18.4), together with the verbal particle *e,* form a future tense with the actor in focus.

> *Ma wai e haere? Ma Pita e haere.*
> Who will go? Peter.

> *Maana e tiihore te hipi.*
> He will skin the sheep.

> *Ma raatou e unahi nga ika.*
> They will scale the fish.

In this construction the actor is the focus constituent of the sentence, and that which is acted upon is the subject. Note that the subject may also be moved forward to precede the verb:

> *Maana te hipi e tiihore. Ma raatou nga ika e unahi.*

24.3 Past actor emphatic with *na . . . i*

The particle *na,* or one of the N-class possessives derived from it (18.4), together with the verbal particle *i,* form a past tense in which the actor is in focus.

24.3

Naana i tiihore te hipi.
He skinned the sheep.

Na te tangata ra i unahi nga ika.
That man scaled the fish.

Naaku i pupuri teenaa tangata.
I detained that man.

As in the previous construction the subject may be moved forward of the predicate:

Naaku teenaa tangata i pupuri. Naana te hipi i tiihore.

24.4 Actor emphatic with *no . . . e . . . ana*

The particle *no,* or one of the N-class possessives derived from it, together with the particles *e . . . ana,* form a continuous tense in which the actor is in focus. This tense is not attested from early Maori texts but is common in contemporary spoken Maori. It occurs only in subordinate clauses.

Noona e tiihore ana i te tia, ka pakuu te puu a Motu.
While he was skinning the deer Motu's gun went off.

No koutou e hari ana i te tangi ka hemo atu te wahine a te kaumaatua.
While you were holding the funeral ceremonies the old man's wife died.

Noona e unahi ana i nga ika ka tiimata ki te ua.
While he was scaling the fish it began to rain.

Noona e whakakii ana i tana kete ka kitea e te tangata.
While he was filling his kit he was discovered.

There are two points to be noticed about this construction. First, it should be noted that it always forms a dependent clause within a sentence. Second, it should be noted that, unlike the future and past agent emphatic, the goal of the verbal phrase in the continuous agent emphatic is introduced by *i.*

24.5 Examples

Ma wai e moe te taane maangere ki te mahi kai? He raa te kai ki taua kiri e-e

Who will marry a man lazy in food production? The sun on her skin would be her (only) food.

Ma wai e moe te wahine, maangere ki te whatu pueru? Ko Tongariro te kai ki taua kiri e-e!

Who will marry a woman lazy at weaving garments? The cold of Tongariro will feed on his skin.

E moohio ana koe ki a Maaui? Naana nei hoki i here te raa; naana anoo hoki i huhuti ake te ika e kiia nei e taatou ko Te Ika a Maaui.

Do you know Maaui? He bound the sun, and fished up the fish which we call the Fish of Maaui (the North Island).

Na te nanakia kahawai ra i kaahaki atu taku paaua.

That rascally *kahawai* has taken my spinner.

25. Negative transforms of nominal sentences

(Examples from this section may be heard on Track 23 of the recordings.)

25.1 Negatives with *ehara . . . i te/a*

25.11 Phrases beginning with *ko, na, no* or any article or definitive

Any phrase beginning with *ko, na, no,* or any article or definitive may be negativised by the negative formula *ehara . . . i te/a*. Note that this formula does not distinguish definiteness versus indefiniteness, singular versus plural, nor the difference between *na* and *no*. However, in those cases where the base has a special plural form (e.g. *tamariki*), this is retained in the negative.

Ko te rangatira teenei. This is the chief.
Ehara teenei i te rangatira. This is not the chief.

He kiwi teeraa manu. That bird is a kiwi.
Ehara teeraa manu i te kiwi. That bird is not a kiwi.

He tamariki raatou. They are children.
Ehara raatou i te tamariki. They are not children.

Na te tangata ra teeraa kurii. That dog belongs to that man.
Ehara teeraa kurii i te tangata ra. That dog does not belong to that man.

No te rangatira teeraa whare. That house is the chief's.
Ehara teeraa whare i te rangatira. That house is not the chief's.

25.12 Examples

Ko Hata pea te rangatira? Ehara a Hata i te rangatira.
Is Hata, perhaps, the chief? Hata is not the chief.

He tangata pai a Matiu? Ehara a Matiu i te tangata pai.
Is Matiu a good man? Matiu is not a good man.

Naau te taiaha e takoto mai ra? Ehara i a au te taiaha ra.
Is the *taiaha* lying there yours? That *taiaha* is not mine.

He waahine eenei? Ehara eenaa i te waahine.
Are these women? Those are not women.

Ko teenei te wahine? Ehara teenaa i te wahine.
Is this the woman? That is not the woman.

He wahine teenei? Ehara teenaa i te wahine.
Is this a woman? That is not a woman.

No Pita teenei? Ehara i a Pita teenaa.
Is this Peter's? That is not Peter's.

Na te waimarie i wini ai maatou. Ehara i te waimarie i wini ai.
We won by luck. It was not by luck.

25.2 Negatives with *kaahore . . . i*

25.21 Phrases beginning with *kei* or *i*
Any phrase beginning with either of the locative particles *kei* or *i* may be negativised by the negative formula *kaahore . . . i*.

Kei konei te tangata. The man is here.
Kaahore te tangata i konei. The man is not here.

I konei te tangata. The man was here.
Kaahore te tangata i konei. The man was not here.

Kei a Pita taku toki. Pita has my axe.
Kaahore taku toki i a Pita. Pita does not have my axe.

I a Pita taku toki. Pita had my axe.
Kaahore taku toki i a Pita. Pita did not have my axe.

Kei nga whare nga manuhiri. The guests are at the houses.
Kaahore nga manuhiri i nga whare. The guests are not at the houses.

25.22 Negatives as verbal sentences

It is of interest to note that *ehara (e hara)*, and *kaahore (ka hore)* can be regarded as verbal phrases, and in fact *hara* 'be wrong' and *hore* 'be nothing, negative' are stative verbs used elsewhere in the language. From this point of view a sentence such as *e hara a Hata i te rangatira* is seen to have the structure of a stative verbal sentence (5.2), i.e. predicate (*e hara*), subject (*a Hata*), comment in *i* (*i te rangatira*), with the literal meaning 'it is wrong that Hata is the chief' or 'Hata is not the chief'. Similarly *Kaahore taku toki i a Pita* can be seen as a stative verbal sentence with predicate (*ka hore*), subject (*taku toki*), comment in *i* (*i a Pita*).

25.3 Negatives with *ehara ma, ehara mo, ehara na, ehara no*

25.31 Actor emphatic construction

Any phrase in *na, no, ma, mo,* including those which are part of an actor emphatic construction (24), may be negativised by preposing *ehara*. Notice that this allows two possible negative forms for constructions beginning with *na* or *no*. The construction *ehara ma/mo/na/no* is an innovation but is now more commonly heard than the *ehara . . . i te* of 25.11

> *Naaku.* Mine.
> *Ehara naaku.* Not mine.
>
> *No Hine.* Hine's.
> *Ehara no Hine.* Not Hine's.
>
> *Ma raatou.* For them.
> *Ehara ma raatou.* Not for them.

25.32 Examples

> *Ehara nooku teenei koti.*
> This coat is not mine.
>
> *Ehara no Hamutana te tangata ra.*
> That man is not from Hamilton.
>
> *Ehara maana nga kai nei.*
> This food is not for him.

Ehara ma Hata e karakia nga kai.
It is not for Hata to say grace.

Ehara mooku teenei whare tino pai.
This very fine house is not for me.

Ehara naaku te taiaha e takoto mai ra.
That *taiaha* lying there is not mine.

Na koutou i hari te tangi, ehara na raatou.
You people led the funeral ceremonies, not them.

Ma raatou e haere te haere; ehara ma maatou.
It is for them to manage it; it is not for us.

26. Time

26.1 Telling the time

The method of telling time is best illustrated by examples:

He aha te taaima?
What is the time?

Ono karaka te taaima.
It is six o'clock.

Rima meneti paahi i te ono karaka.
Five past six o'clock.

Tekau meneti paahi i te ono karaka te taaima.
The time is ten past six.

Koata paahi i te ono karaka te taaima.
It is a quarter past six.

Haawhe paahi i te ono karaka te taaima.
It is half past six.

Rua tekau maa rima meneti ki te whitu karaka te taaima.
It is twenty-five to seven.

Koata ki te whitu karaka te taaima.
It is a quarter to seven.

26.2 'When' past and future

The prepositions *i* and *no* preceding a definitive may indicate past time:

I te ata o taua raa.
On the morning of that day.

No te ahiahi anoo ka haere a Whakatau.
Whakatau went that same evening.

No te matenga o te rangatira ka tangihia te tangi moona.
When the chief died the lament was sung for him.

No tooku taenga ki Waihii ka kite au i a Te Taaite.
When I reached Waihii I saw Te Taaite.

I te haerenga o Tama maa ki Moehau.
When Tama and others went to Moehau.

I na and *no na* are compounded with several locative class bases to form phrases indicating past time:

inapoo, nonapoo 'last night'; *inahea, nonahea* 'when'; *inanahi, nonanahi* 'yesterday'; *inakuanei, nonakuanei* 'a short time ago'

I hea koe inapoo? I te kaainga.
Where were you last night? At home.

Nonahea koe i tae mai ai? Nonanahi nei.
When did you arrive? Yesterday.

The particle *aa* preceding any definitive, or immediately before certain locatives, indicates future time:

Aa hea koe hoki ai? Aapoopoo.
When are you returning? Tomorrow.

Aa te ahiahi ka tiimata te kanikani.
The dance will begin in the evening.

Aaianei 'now'; *aakuanei* 'presently'; *aapoopoo* 'tomorrow'; *aa teeraa ta* 'next year'

26.3 Idioms of time

I te ata-poo 'before dawn'.
  I te ata-poo tonu ka tae mai a Te Tomo.
  Te Tomo arrived before dawn.

I te atatuu 'after sunrise'.
   I te atatuu ka haere maatou ki Te Wairoa.
   After sunrise we left for Te Wairoa.

Te awatea 'middle of the day, broad daylight'.
   Ka awatea, ka kite atu te tamaiti ra i te Kiingi e haere mai ana.
   When it was day the child saw the King approaching.

   Ka tata ki te awatea ka hoki raatou.
   When it was nearly daylight they returned.

Waenganui poo 'middle of the night'
Ao ake te raa 'next day'
Nga rea i mua 'the days gone by, the past'

Te waa kei te haere mai 'the future'
   Ko aa taatou tamariki o naianei ko nga rangatira o te waa kei te haere mai.
   Our children today are the leaders of the future.

I teeraa waa 'at that time'
   I teeraa waa ka haere a Haumoe ki Kaipara.
   At that time Haumoe went to Kaipara.

I nga raa o mua 'in days gone by'.

27. Derived nouns

(Examples from 27.6 may be heard on Track 24 of the recordings.)

27.1 General

Any universal or stative may be transformed into a noun by suffixing the noun derivative suffix. The noun derivative suffix has the following forms: *-nga, -anga, -hanga, -kanga, -manga, -ranga, -tanga,-whanga.*

27.2 Statives select *-nga*

Most statives select the *-nga* alternant of the noun derivative suffix.

27.3 Selection of noun derivative suffix

It is not possible to predict which alternant of the noun derivative suffix will be selected by a particular universal. Worth noting, however, is the relationship between the noun derivative suffix alternant and the passive suffix alternant selected by the same base:

UNIVERSAL	DERIVED NOUN	PASSIVE UNIVERSAL
mahi	*mahinga*	*mahia*
inu	*inumanga*	*inumia*
tangi	*tangihanga*	*tangihia*
noho	*nohoanga*	*nohoia*

If the passive suffix is *-a* the noun derivative suffix will be *-nga;* if the passive suffix is *-ia* the noun derivative suffix will be *-anga.* In all other cases the initial consonant of the passive suffix will be the same as the initial consonant of the noun derivative suffix.

27.4 Meaning of derived nouns

Derived nouns have meanings which may be related to the meaning of the underlying base in either or both of the following ways:

(i) The derived noun may refer to the circumstance, occasion, or time of the action or state expressed by the underlying base. *Moe* is a universal meaning 'to sleep' or 'to marry'. The derived noun *moenga* means 'the occasion of sleeping, marrying'. The universal base *rapu* means 'to seek'. The derived noun *rapunga* means the 'occasion of seeking'. The universal *mahi* means 'work, do'; the derived noun *mahinga* means the 'occasion of working, doing'. The stative *mutu* means 'be ended, finished'. *Mutunga* means 'occasion of ending, finishing'.

(ii) A noun derived from a universal may also refer to some physical object or place associated with the action or state expressed in the underlying base. *Moenga* also means 'bed'; *mahinga* also means 'garden, cultivation'.

27.5 Examples

(The noun derivative suffix is hyphenated in the following examples. It is normally written as part of its word.)

E ara i to moe-nga.
Rise from your bed.

I riro nga whenua Maaori hei noho-anga mo te Paakehaa.
The Maori lands became Pakeha settelements.

Kei whea to moe-nga a Kae?
Where is Kae's sleeping place?

Ko to patu-nga a Maaui i te raa.
Maaui's beating the sun.

Ko te tuutaki-tanga a Pita i a Mere.
Peter's meeting Mary.

I taku tamariki-tanga.
In my childhood.

Kia mau ki to Maaori-tanga.
Hold fast to your Maoriness.

Ta raatou kimi-hanga i te mea ngaro.
Their search for the lost thing.

27.6 Derived nouns used possessively

27.61 Nouns derived from transitive universals

A noun derived from a transitive universal may be possessed either dominantly (taking *a*), or subordinately (taking *o*) according to whether it is derived from an active or a passive universal. Note in the following examples the use of both the comment marker *i* and the passive agent marker *e*:

Taaku patunga i te poaka.
My killing the pig.

Toona patunga e te hoariri.
His being killed by the enemy.

Ta raatou kimihanga i te mea ngaro.
Their search for that which is lost.

Te kitenga tuatahi a Kupe i te whenua hoou.
Kupe's first sighting the new land.

I to raatou tomokanga ki te paa, kaahore he tangata o roto.
When they entered the fort there was no one in it.

27.62 Nouns derived from statives

A noun derived from a stative will always be possessed subordinately (with *o*).

Mahia hei painga moou.
Do it for your own good.

I te matenga o Heremia, ka whakatuuria he teeneti mo te tuupaapaku.
When Heremia died a tent was put up for the body.

I te mutunga o te ua, ka haere maatou ki Kaipara.
When the rain ended we went to Kaipara.

27.63 Nouns derived from intransitive universals

A noun derived from an intransitive universal is possessed by *o*, which is perhaps against our expectations. Study the examples:

No te tau kotahi mano, e iwa rau ma whitu teenei haerenga ooku.
This journey of mine was in 1997.

Te nohoanga o nga manuhiri ka haria atu he kai ma raatou.
The guests sat down and food was brought for them.

Ka noho a Hinewai ki toona nohoanga.
Hinewai sat in her place.

27.7 Examples

Ko taua waahi kaukau he awa wai maaori, he kaukaunga no te tini o te tangata.
That bathing place was a freshwater stream, a bathing place for all the people.

Te moohiotanga o Tama-te-kapua kua kainga ta raaua kurii e Toi ka noho te whakatakariri.
When Tama-te-kapua knew that their dog had been eaten by Toi he was very angry.

Ko te paataitanga iho a Tama, 'E Tuu, kei te ora tonu koe?'
Tama asked, 'Tuu, are you still alive?'

Ko Pararaki te mutunga ake o te one e kiia nei he one roa.
Pararaki is the end of the beach called long beach.

Te taenga o Tuurongo ki Kaawhia ka tahuri ia ki te hanga kaainga moona.
When Tuurongo arrived at Kaawhia he set about building himself a home.

Te kitenga mai a Moeahu i a Te Kowha e haere atu ana, kaatahi anoo ka oma mai. Te tere o te omanga mai!
When Moeahu saw Te Kowha approaching then he ran towards him. How fast he ran!

28. The causative prefix *whaka-* and derived universals

(Examples from this section may be heard on Track 25 of the recordings.)

28.1 General

Universal, noun and stative class bases may take the causative prefix *whaka-*. Nouns and statives are thereby transformed into universals. The class of bases which are already universals remains unchanged.

28.2 Meaning of a universal plus *whaka-*

A universal prefixed by *whaka-* indicates the approach to, attempt at, or causing of the action implied by the simple base. In English the difference is often indicated by the difference in meaning between the same verb used transitively and intransitively; see *tupu* below, for example.

Rongo-hia	hear
whakarongo-hia	listen, cause to hear
kite-a	see
whakakitea	reveal, cause to see
moohio-tia	know
whakamoohio-tia	instruct, warn
noho-ia	sit, dwell
whakanoho-ia	set in place, settle on
tuu-ria	stand
whakatuu-ria	set up
tupu-ria	grow (intransitive)
whakatupu-ria	grow (transitive), rear, foster

28.3 Meaning of nouns and statives plus *whaka-*

Statives and nouns prefixed by *whaka-* will be transformed to universals which indicate the causing of the assumption of the form, condition or state indicated by the simple base.

Tata	be near
whakatata-ngia	approach
kino	be bad
whakakino-tia	debase, make bad
rite	be like, equal
whakarite-a	make like, equal
tika	be straight, correct
whakatika-ngia	make straight, correct
tapu	be sacred, prohibited
whakatapu-a	sanctify, prohibit
ora	be well
whakaora-tia	make well, save
mate	be dead
whakamate-a	kill

28.4 Meaning of locative plus *whaka-*

Whaka- prefixed to locatives gives the meaning 'in the direction of'. Such forms are normally used only as second, qualifying bases in a phrase.

Haere whakamuri	go back
titiro whakawaho	look outwards

Sometimes *whaka-* will be prefixed to a whole phrase as in *whaka-te-tai-tonga* 'towards the south'; *whaka-te-tauranga-waka* 'towards the canoe anchorage'; *ka titiro whaka-te-moana te iwi ra* 'that tribe looked towards the sea'.

28.5 Note on pronunciation

Although written as part of the base, *whaka-* is pronounced, in almost all cases, as if it were a separate unstressed particle. Thus *whakaiti* 'to belittle' does not rhyme with *tamaiti* 'child'. *Whakaiti* is pronounced with the stress on the first *i* of *iti*, since *whaka* is inherently unstressed. In *tamaiti* the stress falls on *ai*, according to the rules for placing stress (54).

In a few words, however, *whaka-* is treated as an integral part of the word for pronunciation purposes. *Whakairo* 'carve' is stressed like *tamaiti* (contrast it with *whakairi* 'to suspend' which is stressed like *whakaiti*). Similarly the word *whakamaa* 'shame' is stressed as though *whaka-* were part of the base, with the stress on the first syllable. (Contrast this with *whakataa* 'to take breath, rest', where the stress is on *taa*.) In the following examples the stress is marked on *whaka-* words by an acute accent.

28.6 Examples

Ka mea a Wairaka, 'Kia whakatáane ake ahau.'
Wairaka said, 'Let me act the part of a man.'

Kaatahi anoo a Rupe ka whakakúukupa i a ia.
Then, for the first time, Rupe turned himself into a pigeon.

Ka tiimata te hoki whakamúri o te toki.
The axe began its return stroke.

Ka takaia te tuupaapaku, ka whakaíria ki runga ki te raakau.
The body was wrapped up and placed up in the tree.

Na wai koe i ako ki te mahi whakáiro?
Who taught you to carve?

Ka whakaréri nga tamariki ki te haere ki Rotorua.
The children got ready to go to Rotorua.

I te iwa o nga haaora i te ata o te Raatapu, ka whakaháeretia te karakia o te Koroneihana.
At nine o'clock on Sunday morning the Coronation Church Service was held.

Ka mea a Hata, 'Kaahore e kore ka wini i a taatou te hiira mo ngaa whakatáetae mahi Maaori.
Hata said, 'There is no doubt that we will win the shield for the Maori Cultural Competition.'

Ka noho ia ki te whakatáa i te manawa.
He sat down to regain his breath.

Nui atu te whákamaa o te tangata ra.
That man was very ashamed.

Waiho ma te whákamaa e patu.
Leave him – let shame punish (him).

29. *Kei* meaning 'lest' or 'don't'

The particle *kei* immediately preposed to a stative or a universal indicates a warning or caveat. Frequently a clause beginning with *kei* will follow a negative imperative beginning with *kaua*. The uses of *kei* are best illustrated with examples.

Kaua e piki raakau kei taka koe!
Don't climb trees lest you fall!

Kia aata koorero taatou kei rongo mai aku hoa.
Let us talk quietly lest my companions hear.

Ka kii atu te waeroa ki te namu, 'Kei riri taaua i te awatea, ka nui te mate.'
The mosquito said to the sandfly, 'Let's not fight (man) in the daylight, or we will be badly defeated.'

Kia aata haere taatou. Kaua e tino tuutata atu ki te taniwha, engari kia tawhiti mai taatou i a ia. Kia tika mai te hau i runga i a ia, kaatahi ka whakatata atu. Kei tika atu te hau i runga i a taatou kei tae atu te piro ki a ia, aa, kei kore e aata takoto aa taatou nei mahi, kei wawe ia te puta ki waho.
Let us go carefully. Don't go too close to the monster, but remain at some distance from him. Let the wind blow directly hither from him, and then approach. Don't let the wind blow from us lest our scent reach him and our work be not completely laid out, and lest he come forth too soon.

Teenei taku koha ki a koe, 'kei hopu to ringa ki te aka taaepa, engari kia mau ki te aka matua.'
This is my parting word to you, 'do not seize hold of the hanging root, but hold fast to the parent root.'

30. The pseudo-verbal continuous with *i te* and *kei te*

(Examples from this section may be heard on Track 26 of the recordings.)

30.1 Explanation

The locative prepositions *kei* 'present position' and *i* 'past position' are frequently used in conjunction with *te* 'singular definite article' and a universal or stative base to form a construction with the same meaning as the continuous tense formed with *e . . . ana* (8.2), and conveniently translated by the '-ing' tense in English.

Note, however, that while the *e . . . ana* construction may refer to present, past or future, *i te* refers definitely to the past only, while *kei te* refers to the present or future.

30.2 Examples

Kei te aha a Hata?
What is Hata doing?

Kei te koorero ia.
He is talking.

Kei te whakatoi tonu a Rewi ki a Tamahae.
Rewi is still teasing Tamahae.

Kei te haere koutou ki Poihaakena aapoopoo.
You will be going to Sydney tomorrow.

I te aha nga tamariki inanahi?
What were the children doing yesterday?

I te taakaro nga tamariki inanahi.
The children were playing yesterday.

30.3

30.3 Pseudo-verbal passives

Notice that universals in pseudo-verbal constructions may be used actively or passively:

Kei te kataina a Rewi e Tamahae.
Rewi is being laughed at by Tamahae.

30.4 Dialectal variation

30.41 Pseudo-verbal continuous in the eastern dialect area

The pseudo-verbal continuous is an extremely common construction in the eastern dialect area where it largely replaces the *e . . . ana* tense of the western dialect area, which includes North Auckland and all of the North Island west of the Central Plateau and ranges.

30.42 *Kei to aha koe?*

Among most eastern tribes a common greeting is *kei te peewhea koe?* 'how are you ?' Ngaati-Porou, however, say *kei te aha koe?* 'how are you?' which would mean elsewhere 'what are you doing?' In North Auckland *e peehea ana koe?* (shortened to *peeha-ana koe?*) is more usual.

30.43 Pronunciation of *kei*

Kei is pronounced, and sometimes written, *kai* by most eastern dialect speakers and also in the Wanganui River area.

30.5 Negative of pseudo-verbal constructions

As stated earlier (25.21) any phrase beginning with the locative particles *kei* or *i* is negativised by *kaahore . . . i.*

Kei te kuti hipi a Paeko. Kaahore a Paeko i te kuti hipi.
Paeko is shearing sheep. Paeko is not shearing sheep.

Kei te purei kaari nga taangata. Kaahore nga taangata i te purei kaari.
The people are playing cards. The people are not playing cards.

Kei a Hata te hooiho o Paeko. Kaahore te hooiho o Paeko i a Hata.
Hata has Paeko's horse. Hata does not have Paeko's horse.

Kei Pooneke raatou e noho ana. Kaahore raatou i Pooneke e noho ana.
They are living at Wellington. They are not living in Wellington.

Kaahore a Tamahae i te whakarongo ki a Hata ma.
Tamahae is not listening to Hata and the others.

Kaahore a Tamahae raaua ko Rewi i te miraka kau tonu.
Tamahae and Rewi were not still milking the cows.

31. Complex phrases

31.1 Definition, discussion and examples

Complex phrases are those phrases which contain more than one base e.g. *te whare hoou* 'the new house'. In theory there is no limit to the number of bases a phrase may contain. In practice two-base phrases are very common, three-base phrases are quite common, and there are occasional instances of phrases containing more than three bases. In every case it is helpful to regard the nucleus of a complex phrase as containing two slots, the first slot being filled by a single base which is modified (qualified) by the base or bases which fill the second slot.

Te wahine aataahua.
The beautiful woman.

Te tangata pai.
The good man.

Nga marae huinga taangata.
The meeting grounds of people.

Nga kamupene kanataraka mahi rooku.
The logging contracting companies.

I tangi tuu te wahine.
The woman wept standing.

E tangi hotu ana te wahine.
The woman is weeping (with sobs).

Ka tangi haere te wahine.
The woman weeps as she goes along.

Ka rere tiitaha te manu.
The bird flies from side to side.

31.2 Nouns in the second slot of verbal phrases

It should be noted that in complex phrases nouns may fill the second slot in verbal phrases although, by definition, a noun does not stand as the only base in a verbal phrase.

E kai pia ana nga taurekareka ra.
Those scoundrels are drinking beer.

Kei to ruku kooura nga iwi of te kaainga.
The people of the village are diving for crayfish.

He patu hipi te mahi i teeraa wheketere.
Slaughtering sheep is the work in that factory.

E kohi pipi ana nga tamariki i taatahi.
The children are gathering pipis at the beach.

He kato waatakirihi te mahi it te repo.
Picking watercress is the work in the swamp.

He whaiwhai poaka te mahi a nga taane.
Pig-hunting is the occupation of the men.

Ka mutu te miraka kau ka haere nga tamariki ki te hii ika.
After milking the cows the children will go fishing.

32. The uses and meanings of *i* and *ki* in non-initial phrases

(Examples from this section may be heard on Track 27 of the recordings.)

32.1 General

I and *ki* are particles of extremely frequent occurrence, both of which are used in various constructions, and with differences of meaning which can be very puzzling to the learner. In this section some effort is made to sort out and describe the functions of these two particles when they occur in non-initial phrases, that is to say, in the comment of a sentence (38.4).

32.2 *Ki* meaning 'towards'

Ki has the basic meaning 'in the direction of, towards', and this meaning is inherent in most of its uses, even when actual motion is not involved.

32.21 *Ki* after active universals connoting motion

After universals clearly connoting motion such as *haere* 'go', *hoki* 'return', *tomo* 'enter', *oma* 'run', *rere* 'fly', a comment in *ki* indicates the goal of the action, and *ki* can be translated 'to, towards'.

E hoki ana au ki te kaainga.
I am going to the village.

Tomo mai ki te whare!
Come into the house!

Hoki atu ki to whenua!
Go back to your country!

Ka rere a Tainui ki taawaahi o te moana.
Tainui sailed to the other side of the ocean.

32.22 Pseudo-motion

With many universals which do not connote actual motion, we can nevertheless readily conceive of the action being 'directed' towards a goal. After such universals as *titiro* 'look', *karanga* 'call', *tangi* 'weep', *whawhai* 'fight', *mahara* 'remember, recall', *paatai* 'question, ask', the comment is usually introduced by *ki* if it is a goal which is separate from the actor. If the action is reflexive, however, as in 'asking a question', 'thinking a thought', the comment will be introduced by *i*.

Ka titiro mai ia ki tooku kaakahu.
He looks towards my garment.

E mahara tonu ana au ki oo taaua tuutakitanga i nga waa o mua.
I am continually recalling our meetings in days gone by.

32.23 Selection of *ki* where motion does not seem to be involved

In a number of cases universals select *ki* as goal-marker when it is difficult for English speakers to conceive of motion or direction being involved. The bases *moohio* 'know', *hiahia* 'desire', *piirangi* 'desire', *whakapono* 'believe', *whakaae* 'agree', *whakahee* 'disagree', all usually occur with *ki* as goal-marker.

E moohio ana au ki a ia.
I know him.

Ka nui tana hiahia ki te wahine ra.
Great is his desire for that woman.

E whakahee ana au ki ta raatou koorero.
I disagree with what they say.

32.24 Pseudo-verbal goals of universals and statives: the so-called infinitive

After a verbal phrase containing an active universal or a stative base a comment in *ki* may be suitably translated by an English infinitive.

Kua hoki ia ki te moe.
He has gone back to sleep.

Ka tata ia ki te mate.
He is close to death (dying).

Kua haere ia ki te inu.
He has gone to drink.

Naana te tamaiti nei i ako ki te waiata.
He taught the child to sing.

32.25 The instrumental comment with *ki*

After a passive verbal phrase a comment introduced by *ki* denotes the instrument by means of which the action was performed. 'With, by' are appropriate translations.

Ka topea te raakau ki te toki.
The tree is chopped down with the axe.

Ka kitea te tangata ki nga tapuwae.
The man was found by his footprints.

Teeraa pea e haoa e Te Whaanau-a-Apanui ki te kupenga, te tere kahawai ra.
Perhaps that school of kahawai will be caught by Te Whaanau-a-Apanui with a net.

An active verbal phrase may also take an instrumental comment in *ki*, but in this case a comment in *i* must also be present. *Ka tope ia i te raakau ki te toki* 'he fells the tree with the axe'.

32.3 The functions of *i* in non-initial phrases

It is not possible to suggest a basic meaning which will cover all of the uses of *i* in its broad function as comment marker, but in the following sections an attempt is made to distinguish what, to the English speaker at least, appear to be different meanings of *i*, and to suggest appropriate translations in different environments.

32.31 *I* after active universals not connoting motion

After an active universal not connoting the idea of motion a comment introduced by *i* will indicate the goal of the action. Such a goal will be translated either by a direct object in English, as in *ka hanga raatou i te whare* 'they built the house', or by a prepositional phrase as in *ka moe raatou i te whare* 'they slept at the house'. Notice that although the English translations differ the Maori structure remains the same.

Ka noho teeraa tangata i toona whare.
That man dwelt at his house.

Kei te tiki a Rewi i nga kaawhe.
Rewi is fetching the calves.

Kei te patu a Tamahae i nga kau.
Tamahae is hitting the cows.

Kaahore taua wahine i kite i te hiku o te taniwha.
That woman did not see the monster's tail.

Kua rongo iho te wahine nei i te kaha o te ngongoro o te ihu.
The woman heard the strength of the snoring.

E tupu ana nga puu wiiwii i te taha maui.
The clumps of rushes are growing on the left side.

32.32 *I* after universals connoting motion

After a universal connoting motion a comment in *i* will usually translate as 'from', there being in such cases a clear contrast between *ki* 'towards' and *i* 'away from'.

I haere mai au ki te whare.
I came to the house.

I haere mai au i te whare.
I came from the house.

32.33 *I* after statives

After a stative *i* may indicate either (a) that which is responsible for the state

115

or condition indicated by the base, in which case it can be translated 'by, because of', or (b) the position or place at which the condition or state came about, when 'at, in, on, from' are appropriate translations.

(a) *Ka riro i te kahawai nui tana paaua.*
     His paua-shell spinner was carried off by the big kahawai.

     Ka paa te aawangawanga ki te taane kei riro tana tamaiti i te iwi o te moana.
     The husband became anxious lest his child be carried off by the people of the sea.

     Pau atu a Toi me Uenuku, me to raaua iwi i te ahu.
     Toi and Uenuku and their people were consumed by fire.

     Ka haehae a Parewhete i nga ringa ki te mataa kia heke iho ai nga toto ki runga i a Wairangi, kia tapu ai i ana toto, kia kore e kainga.
     Parewhete slashed her arms with flint so that the blood would flow over Wairangi and he would be made sacred by her blood and not eaten.

(b) *Ka putu raaua i te waharoa o te marae.*
     They appeared at the gateway of the marae.

     E maany mai ana te takere i te kare of te moana.
     The hull was floating on the waves of the sea.

33. The imperative with statives

(Examples from this section may be heard on Track 28 of the recordings.)

33.1 Affirmative imperative with statives

The imperative of stative bases is formed by the verbal particle *kia* and imperative intonation:

Kia kaha! kia toa! kia manawa-nui!
Be strong! be brave! be steadfast!

Kia tere!
Be quick!

Kia ngaawari!
Be obedient!

Kia tuupato!
Be careful!

Kia uu!
Be firm!

Kia pai taatou ki a taatou!
Let us be good to each other!

Kia kaha te whakaaro!
Think hard!

33.2 Negative imperative with statives

A negative imperative, usually with a sense of warning, can be formed by the particle *kei* before a stative:

Kei whara koe!
Don't get hurt!

Kei mate koe!
Don't get killed (look out)!

Kei taka koe!
Don't fall down!

Kei kaha te pupuri i nga mea na!
Don't hold those things too tight!

34. Subordinate clauses with *kia*

(Examples from this section may be heard on Track 29 of the recordings.)

34.1 Different-actor subordination

We may regard a complex sentence such as 'we come here so that you will learn Maori' as being derived from two simple sentences 'we come here' and 'you will learn Maori'. In combination we say that 'we come here' is the main sentence (or clause) and 'so that you will learn Maori' is the subordinate sentence (or clause). In the example given you should notice that the actor in the main sentence 'we' is different from the actor in the subordinate sentence 'you' and we will refer to such a situation as 'different actor'. We can now state the rule that 'in Maori a different-actor subordinate sentence takes a verbal phrase in *kia*.' Our Maori sentence will be *ka haere mai taaua ki konei kia ako koe i te reo Maaori.* Other examples follow:

Haere mai taaua kia kite koe i nga puna wai e rua.
Let us two go so that you may see the two springs of water.

E kore koe e pai kia haere au ki toou kaainga?
Wouldn't you like me to come to your place?

Ka karangatia mai maatou kia haere.
We were called to go.

Ka haere taatou ki te paa kia kite au i aku tamariki.
We will go to the village so that I may see my children.

34.2 *Ai* in different-actor subordinate sentences

In order to indicate that the action or state in the subordinate sentence is a result of the action in the main sentence postpose *ai* to the verbal phrase of the subordinate sentence.

Ka haere mai taaua ki konei kia ako ai koe i te reo Maaori.
We come here so that you will learn Maori (accordingly).

Tooia ake te tatau kia uru mai ai te hauhau ki a au.
Pull open the door so that the breeze will blow on me.

119

35. The proper article *a*

(Examples from this section may be heard on Track 30 of the recordings.)

35.1 With locatives and personals

The proper article *a* occurs with personals and locatives in the following circumstances:

(i) with locatives and personals (except personal pronouns) when they stand as subject (38.3).

(ii) with personals (including all personal pronouns except *ahau*) when they follow *ki, i, kei, hei.*

35.2 Pronunciation note

Before the pronouns *koe* and *ia* the proper article is lengthened to *aa* and takes the phrase stress, thus *ki aa koe, ki aa ia.* Before the personal pronoun *au* the proper article coalesces with the first vowel of the pronoun, thus *aau.* The combination *a au* is homophonous with (sounds the same as) *aau* 'your' (plural form of *taau*) but a distinction is maintained in writing.

35.3 Examples

(i) *He maania a Kaingaroa.*
Kaingaroa is a plain.

He mea puhipuhi a runga ki te puhi kereruu.
The top was adorned with pigeon feathers.

E puare katoa ana a roto.
All the inside was hollow.

Teeraa a waho te kai tahi ra; teeraa a roto he hahae kee ra.
Outwardly (they) eat together; inwardly they are jealous (of each other).

Ka mea atu a Tinirau.
Tinirau said.

Ka titiro a Kae.
Kae looked.

(ii) *Ka kite atu ia i a Paania.*
He saw Paania.

He tauranga tapu teeraa i te waa i a raatou.
That was a protected fishing-ground in their time.

Hoomai ki a au!
Give (it) to me!

36. The continuative particle *ana*

(Examples from this section may be heard on Track 31 of the recordings.)

36.1 The imperfect with *e . . . ana*

Ana occurs in the postposed periphery of verbal phrases, in the position following the directive particles. It is worth noting that *ana* is incompatible with (cannot occur in the same phrase with) the positional particles *nei, na, ra* (3).

A verbal phrase with *e* in the preposed periphery and *ana* postposed indicates a continuing action or state. The -ing tense in English is an appropriate translation. *E haere atu ana te tangata* 'the man is/was going away'.

36.2 Dialectal note

The *e . . . ana* tense is particularly characteristic of the western dialect area, and especially Northland. In the eastern dialect area it is usually replaced by the pseudo-verbal construction with *kei te* and *i te* (30).

36.3 Narrative style with *ana*

Ana is frequently postposed in verbal phrases which have no preposed verbal particle. This usage marks narrative style. Appropriate translation is suggested by the context.

Ka haere atu a Kae i a Hine raaua ko Rau, ka tae ki to raaua kaainga. Na, kawea ana e raatou a Kae, ka whakatakotoria ki te pou tokomanawa o te whare o Tinirau.

Kae went with Hine and Rau and arrived at their home. Then Kae was carried and laid down by them at the main supporting post of Tinirau's house.

36.4 Passage illustrating the uses of *ana*

Ka mahara te wahine ra kua mate toona taane; haere ana ki te rapu, ka kitea ia e takoto ana, kua mate – kaaore i mate rawa. Wahaa ana e ia ki too raaua whare, ka horoia oona patunga. Ka haere te wahine ki te tiki wahie, ka mea atu a Taawhaki, 'Ka kite koe i te raakau roa e tuu ana, turakina, ka amo mai.'

The woman thought that her husband was dead. She went to seek and found him lying injured, but not dead. She carried him to their home and bathed his wounds. Then the woman went to fetch firewood. Tawhaki said, 'You will see a tall tree standing. Fell it and carry it back here.'

36.5 Conditional tense with *ka . . . ana*

Ana postposed in a phrase with *ka* preposed forms a conditional tense which must be dependent on a further verbal phrase beginning with *ka*.

Ka haere ana koe, ka mahue pani maatou.
If you go we will be left like orphans.

Ka riri ana te tangata ra, ka tetee oona niho.
When that man gets angry he grinds his teeth.

Ka haere mai ana te Kuiini ki Niu Tiireni, ka aituaa te iwi Maaori.
Whenever the Queen comes to New Zealand the Maori people suffer a disaster.

36.6 *Kei . . . ana* means 'while'

Me haere taatou kei pai ana te raa.
Let's go while it's fine.

Mahia nga mahi kei tamariki ana.
Get things done while (you're) young.

I te waa i mua ra, kei hine ana au.
In time gone by, when I was a girl.

36.7 Exclamatory style with *ana*

Aroha ana ki te whakarongo atu!
(It) was pitiful to listen to!

Pai ana ki te koorero atu!
(It) was good to say!

Hoohaa ana ki te whakatuu!
(It) was tiresome to set up!

Rere kee ana ki te titiro atu!
(It) was strange to see!

Kino ana ki te whakarongo atu!
(It) was horrible to listen to!

37. Interjections and interjectory phrases

There is a small set of bases and phrases which occur at the beginning of sentences with exclamatory intonation. A selection of these interjections and interjectory phrases is treated in the following subsections.

37.1 Interjections

37.11 *Na* 'now, then, and'
Na is very commonly used in animated narrative:

> *Na, ka tere haere nei a Hinauri i te moana.*
> And Hinauri floated along on the sea.

> *Na, ka rewa te ope a Ngaati Awa.*
> Then the party of Ngaati Awa set forth.

37.12 *Kaatahi* 'then', *kaatahi anoo* 'then, for the first time, at last, just'
Notice that in sentences beginning with *kaatahi* (*anoo*) the subject, especially if a pronoun, will often precede the predicate and the verbal phrase will usually take the verbal particle *ka:*

> *Kaatahi ia ka hoki atu ki te kaainga.*
> Then he returned home.

> *Kaatahi anoo au kua tae mai.*
> I have just arrived (or I have arrived at last, or I have arrived for the first time).

> *Kaatahi ka tae te rongo ki nga iwi katoa.*
> Then the news reached all the tribes.

37.13 *Aa* 'and (after some time), and so'
The intonation associated with this word marks hesitation or pause rather

37.13

than exclamation. In writing it should be set off by commas:

Aa, i muri iho i taua tautohetanga ka mea mai a Taranga.
And, soon after that argument Taranga said.

Ka utaina nga utanga o ia waka, o ia waka, aa, ka ruupeke ki runga me nga taangata.
The cargo was loaded on each canoe and then everything was assembled on board including the people.

37.14 *Anoo* 'as if, like'
Pronounced *aanoo* by some speakers:

Anoo ko te whetuu ka puta ake i te pae, nga karu o te tangata ra.
It was as if a star was appearing above the horizon—the eyes of that man.

Ko te kanohi, anoo he rangi raumati.
(Her) face was like a summer's day.

Te putanga ake o te raa, anoo he ahi e toro ana ki te whenua.
The rising of the sun was like a fire spreading across the earth.

37.15 *Anaa!, Anana!* 'behold'

Anaa! Ka wehi taua iwi ki oona kanohi.
Behold, those people were frightened by his eyes.

Anana! Kaatahi ka aata haere taua maaia nei, a Tama-nui-te-raa.
Behold, now that rascal the sun goes slowly.

37.16 *Otiraa!* 'however, but'

Otiraa! Naana anoo i mea kia paa ia i te koohatu a toona paapaa.
But it was he himself who decided that he should be struck by the stone (thrown by) his father.

Noona anoo taua kaainga; otiraa, no maatou katoa.
That place is his own; however it belongs to us all.

37.17 *Taihoa!* 'wait a while'

Taihoa taatou e haere!
Let us wait a while before we go.

Taihoa, Tamahae!
Wait, Tamahae!

37.18 *Kaitoa!* 'it serves you right'

Kaitoa koe kia mate!
Serves you right that you were beaten.

37.2 Interjctory phrases

37.21 *Heoti (anoo), heoi (anoo)* 'accordingly, as a result'

Heoi ka mate a Maaui. Otiraa, mate rawa ake ia, kua tupu oona uri.
And so Maaui died; he died but his descendants multiplied.

Heoti anoo ka haere raatou.
Accordingly they went.

Heoti anoo ka ea te mate o Tuu-whakararo.
As a result the death of Tuu-whakararo was avenged.

37.22 *Koia (anoo), koia nei (koinei), koia na (koina), koia ra (koira),* 'indeed, it is the case that, here is,' etc.

Koia pea teenaa? Aae koia anoo.
Perhaps that is the one? Yes, that's it.

Koina te take i kitea mai ai ahau, he whai mai i taku paaua.
That is the reason why I am here, (I) sought my fishing-lure.

E kore koia koe e pai mai ki taku tuahine hei wahine maau?
Would you not like my sister as your wife?

37.22

Koina tonu he tohu ma koorua.
Here indeed is a sign for you two.

37.23 Greetings and farewells

The conventional Maori greetings are *kia ora!* and *teenaa koe (koorua, koutou).* When saying goodbye the person who is leaving says *hei konei!* 'remain here' or *e noho ra!* 'remain there'. The person who is staying says *haere ra!* 'go then!'

37.24 *Naawai, aa* 'and after a time'

Naawai, aa, ka nui noa atu toona rongo, pakuu ana ki nga iwi katoa.
And after a time his fame became very great, resounding among all the tribes.

Naawai, aa, ka mimiti noa iho te mano ra.
And after a time the multitude diminished.

37.25 *Ina ake anoo, ina hoki (ra)* 'and so, hence, since'

Ina ake anoo i haere ai te rongo o teenei wahine.
And so the fame of this woman spread.

Wheetero atu ana te arero o te tangata wero. Ina hoki ra tana ariki.
The ceremonial challenger's tongue protruded in the *wheetero.* For this was his high chief!

38. The structure of the simple verbal sentence

38.1 General

Throughout this course emphasis has been laid on the importance of the phrase as a grammatical unit in Maori. As we have seen, Maori utterances are arrangements of phrases, each of which consists of a central nucleus containing the lexical information, and peripheral particles which add grammatical information. The grammatical information added by the peripheral particles is of two main kinds: firstly, that which defines the meaning of the nucleus, and secondly, that which relates the phrase, as a whole, to other phrases in the sentence. As an example of the first kind of information we may consider the meanings of the various articles *te, nga, he, a,* all of which tell us something more about the meaning of the nucleus of the phrase in which they occur.

The function of the phrase in a sentence (the second kind of grammatical information mentioned above) can be indicated either by the initial particle of the phrase, or by the position of the phrase in the sentence, or by both. In the sentence *ka tahia te kaainga e Rupe* 'the home was swept out by Rupe', the function of the agentive phrase is indicated by its initial particle *e.* In the sentence *ko te oranga o tana ahi i whiua e ia ki te kaikoomako* 'the remnants of the fire were cast by him into the *kaikoomako* tree' the function of each phrase is marked by its initial particle, but the phrase *ko te oranga* is marked as the focus of the sentence twice, firstly by the particle *ko,* and secondly by its position at the beginning of the sentence. It is probably for this reason that *ko* may be omitted in this position without altering the meaning of the utterance at all.

Phrases may fulfil any of four functions in a sentence: subject, predicate, comment or interjection. A phrase (or combination of phrases) which fulfils one of these functions is said to be a constituent of the sentence. The four types of sentence constituent are considered in the following sections.

38.2 The predicate

The predicate of a simple verbal sentence is always a verbal phrase (1.2). Usually, but not always, the predicate occurs at the beginning of a sentence. In the following examples the predicate is indicated by roman type:

Ka haere *a Maaui ki te hii ika.*
Maaui went to fish.

He aha ra i mau eke ai *te ika ki tana matau.*
Why were the fish caught by his hook?

38.3 The subject

The subject of a simple verbal sentence is the nominal phrase that does not begin with a preposition (17). The subject phrase is said to be unmarked. It will begin with a definitive or, when the subject is in focus (38.31), with *ko.* In the following sentences the subject is marked, in each case, by bold type.

*Kaatahi ka karanga mai **te whaanau a Taane**.*
Then the family of Taane called out.

*Ka hoki anoo **a Rata** ki te tarai i tana waka.*
Rata returned to adze out his canoe.

*Ka moe **a Wahie-roa** i a Kura.*
Wahie-roa married Kura.

*Ka maminga **raatou** i te raakau a Rata.*
They interfered with Rata's tree.

*Kua haere **te tamaiti** ki te kaukau.*
The child has gone to bathe.

38.31 Subject in focus

Emphasis may be placed on the subject of a sentence by moving it to the beginning and preposing the focus particle *ko.* The subject is then said to be 'in focus' or 'focused'. The subject is focused in the sentence *ko Mahuika i ngaro tonu iho* 'Mahuika was immediately destroyed.' The normal order would be *i ngaro tonu iho a Mahuika.* In the following examples the subject in focus is in bold type.

__Ko nga raakau anake__ i tupu tonu.
Only the trees continued to grow.

Ka mea a Rata, __'ko koutou anoo__ e maminga nei i taku raakau.'
Rata said, 'It is you who are interfering with my tree.'

__Ko Rata anake__ i eke atu ki uta.
Rata alone went ashore.

__Ko Wahieroa__ kua moe i a Kura.
Wahieroa has married Kura.

__Ko Aotea__ i tukua atu ki a Rongorongo.
Aotea was given to Rongorongo.

38.4 The comment

The comment is usually non-initial in the sentence. It may begin with any of the prepositions *ki, i, hei, kei, e* 'agentive', *na, no, ma, mo* (but not *me* 'and', *o, a* 'of'). In the following examples the comment is in bold type.

Ka haere a Maaui __ki te hii ika__.
Maaui went to fish.

Kaaore te ika i mau __i tana matau__.
The fish were not caught by his hook.

Ka moe a Wahieroa __i a Kura__.
Wahieroa married Kura.

He pukapuka __naaku__ teenei.
This is a book belonging to me.

Ka koorerotia __e te wahine ra__ te aahua o te tangata ra.
The woman told the appearance of that man.

38.5 Conjunctive phrases

Conjunctive phrases begin with the prepositions *a, o, me.* They are always part of a constituent, never the whole. In the sentence *kei whea te waka me te hoe?* 'where is the canoe and the paddle?' which consists of a focus and a subject, the subject constituent is *te waka me te hoe.* The unity of this constituent is indicated in normal speech by the fact that the possible pause between the two phrases *te waka* and *me te hoe* is not, in fact, realised. Every phrase beginning with *a, o* 'of' or *me* 'and' is similarly part of a constituent:

Ka koorero a Pita ki nga mema o te komiti.
Peter spoke to the members of the committee.

Koia na te mate o te kuuware, kaaore e moohio he aha te aha.
That's the trouble with being ignorant; you don't know what is what.

Tapahia nga peka me nga rau o te raakau.
Chop off the branches and the foliage of the tree.

38.6 The interjection

An interjection constituent of a sentence consists either of an interjectory phrase such as *kaatahi anoo* 'now for the first time', or a vocative phrase such as *e hoa!* 'friend!', or a single base of the interjection class, such as *inana!* 'behold!'

Kaatahi *te rangi aataahua!*
What a beautiful day!

Naa, *ka hangaa e Whakaue he pourewa moona.*
Now, Whakaue built himself a stage.

Teenaa, *tirohia te aahua o teenei whare!*
Now then, look at the appearance of this house!

38.7 Constituents in apposition

Two constituents beginning with the same initial particle are in apposition, that is to say, they fulfil the same function in the sentence. *Ka rapu a Maaui i tana whaea, i a Taranga.* 'Maaui looked for his mother, Taranga.' This sentence has two comments in apposition. The following sentence has three focuses in apposition: *ko te poo nui, ko te poo roa, ko te poo whakaau te moe* 'the great night, the long night, the night of deep sleep.'

> *Kei te moohio au ki to matua, ki a Whairiri.*
> I know your father, Whairiri.

> *Ko te uunga mai o Tainui, o te waka i uu tuatahi mai.*
> The landing of Tainui, the first canoe to land.

> *Ka kitea a Maaui ki te ngaro, ki nga manu e karamui ana i runga i a ia.*
> Maaui was found because of the flies and birds which swarmed over him.

> *Ao ake anoo te raa kua whakatika a Taranga, kua ngaro whakarere i te whare.*
> As soon as it was day Taranga had arisen and was quickly gone from the house.

> *I haehae rawa iho raatou ki roto i te puku nui o te taniwha. E noho-a-tinana tonu ana te wahine, te tamariki, te taane. Ko eetahi anoo kua motu i te pane, i nga ringa, i nga wae raanei, no te komenga pea o nga ngutu, no te whakatanukutanga o te korokoro.*
> They cut right down into the great belly of the monster. Men, women and children were still recognisable in there. Some had their heads cut off, some were severed in the middle, or at the arms, or the legs, from the munching of the jaws perhaps, or from the swallowing action of the throat.

38.8 Multiple constituents

A simple sentence may contain more than one constituent of the same kind without their being in apposition. In the sentence *ka topea te raakau e te tangata ki te toki* 'the tree was cut down by the man with the axe' there are two comments, namely the agentive phrase *e te tangata* and the instrumental phrase *ki te toki*. In *kawea atu te mea na ki te tangata i te whare ra* 'take that thing to the man in that house' there are also two comments, the directional phrase *ki te tangata* and the locational phrase *i te whare*.

In the sentence *ka rongo teetahi wahine no runga i te rangi ki te toa o Taawhaki* 'a certain woman up in the sky heard of Taawhaki's bravery' there are two comments, each of which consists of two phrases. They are *no runga i te rangi* and *ki te toa o Taawhaki*. The latter is a single constituent because *o* can initiate only conjunctive phrases which are never whole constituents. The former is a single constituent because the *i* of the second phrase follows a locative (38.6).

39. *No te* and its various meanings

(Examples from this section may be heard on Track 32 of the recordings.)

39.1 *No te* means 'when'

The reference is to the point of time in the past at which an action took place:

> *No te ahiahi ka haere a Whakatau.*
> Whakatau left in the evening.

> *No te tau kotahi mano, e iwa rau maa whitu, teenei haerenga ooku.*
> This journey of mine was in the year nineteen hundred and seven.

> *No teetahi poo kei te purupuru a Maaui i te matapihi, i te whatitoka o too raatou whare.*
> One night Maaui stuffed up the window and the door of their house.

> *Kaatahi ia ka aata titiro i te takahanga waewa – no te poo noa atu teenei mahinga, ehara i te ata nei.*
> Then he looked carefully at the footsteps – this was something done the night before, not this morning.

39.2 *No te* with derived nouns

A pseudo-verbal construction is formed with *no te* peripheral to a noun derived from either a universal or a stative. This construction is usually found in focus position at the beginning of the sentence. Reference is to the point of time in the past when the action or condition referred to by the verbal noun was occurring.

> *No te horonga o Mokoia ka riro nga wheua o Tuuhourangi i a Ngaapuhi.*
> The bones of Tuuhourangi were taken away by Ngaapuhi at the time when Mokoia was captured.

> *No te taenga ki te raumati, ka mahana te kiri o te tangata.*
> When summer arrived people began to feel warm.

No te matenga o Hawe-pootiki, ka pokaia e Turi te manawa.
When Hawe-pootiki was dead Turi cut out his heart.

No te haerenga ka paakia te ringaringa o Haakawau ki te paepae o te whare.
When he left Haakawau slapped his hand against the threshold of the house.

No te mutunga o te tangihanga, ka kiia atu e Rehua, 'Tahuna he ahi.'
When the greeting was done, Rehua said, 'Light a fire.'

39.3 *No te . . . ai* means 'because'

No te katanga a Tiiwaiwaka i a Maaui i kuutia ai e Hine-nui-te-poo, aa, mate ana.
It was because Fantail laughed at Maaui that (he) was crushed by Hine-nui-te-poo and died.

No te tangi ka maatau ai a Rehua ko toona teina teenei.
Rehua knew from the lament that this was his junior relative.

40. Reduplication

40.1 General

Reduplication is of three kinds, full reduplication, as *wera, werawera*, partial reduplication, as in *pango, papango*, and infixed reduplication, as in *tangata, taangata*.

40.2 Complete reduplication

In most cases complete reduplication of a base indicates that the action, or state, is of frequent or continued occurrence.

> *Mate* 'to die', *matemate* 'die in numbers'
> *paki* 'pat', *pakipaki* 'pat frequently, clap'
> *kimo* 'wink', *kimokimo* 'wink frequently, blink'

Sometimes full reduplication of a stative diminishes its intensity.

> *Wera* 'hot', *werawera* 'warm'
> *mate* 'sick', *matemate* 'sickly'

40.3 Partial reduplication

In some cases partial reduplication indicates a single terminal action.

> *kimo* 'wink', *kikimo* 'shut the eyes'
> *paki* 'pat', *papaki* 'slap or clap once'

In other cases partial reduplication indicates diminished intensity.

> *Maaroo* 'hard, stiff', *maarooroo* 'somewhat hard, stiff'
> *pango* 'black', *papango* 'somewhat black'
> *whero* 'red', *whewhero* 'reddish'

40.3

In a few cases an adjective in the qualifying slot of the nucleus is partially reduplicated (optionally), to indicate that the base in the first nucleus slot is plural.

He raakau nunui 'big trees'
he raakau roroa 'tall trees'
he raakau papai 'good trees'

40.4 Infixed reduplication

In the following seven words a vowel is doubled to indicate plurality.

te tangata 'the man', *nga taangata* 'the men'
te wahine 'the woman', *nga waahine* 'the women'
te tupuna 'the ancestor', *nga tuupuna* 'the ancestors'
te tuakana 'the older sibling', *nga tuaakana* 'the older siblings'
te teina 'the younger sibling', *nga teeina* 'the younger siblings'
te matua 'the parent', *nga maatua* 'the parents'
te tuahine 'the sister', *nga tuaahine* 'the sisters'

40.5 Examples

(The following examples may be heard on Track 33 of the recordings.)

Hoomai te pakipaki.
Give (him) a good hand!

E whiowhio haere ana te tangata.
The man is going along whistling.

No hea to mana? No ooku tuupuna.
Where does your mana come from? From my ancestors.

Kei hea nga maatua o eenei tamariki?
Where are the parents of these children?

Ko ta raaua nei mahi taakaro he whakatangitangi puu toorino.
Their hobby was flute-playing.

I nga waa e huihui ana nga hapuu o Rotorua ki Mokoia ka kitea a Hinemoa i waenganui o toona iwi.
While the tribes of Rotorua were assembling at Mokoia Hinemoa was seen in the midst of her people.

Ko te amuamu te tino rongoa a te Paakehaa hei patu i nga ture e kinongia e raatou.
Grumbling is the best remedy of Europeans for putting down laws which are disliked by them.

E hikohiko ana te uira i runga i nga pae maunga.
The lightning is flashing above the mountain ridges.

Kua pau te kai a nga hoa, katikati tonu ana a Tama-te-kapua.
His friends have finished their food but Tama-te-kapua nibbles on.

Ko wai teenaa e maatakitaki mai ana ki a maatou?
Who is that looking at us?

I te ahiahi ka tiimata te hokihoki o nga taangata ki oo raatou whare.
In the evening the people began to return to their houses.

41. The biposed particle *anoo*

(Examples from this section may be heard on Track 34 of the recordings.)

41.1 *Anoo* as a postposed particle

As a postposed particle *anoo* may occur both in verbal and nominal phrases. When postposed it occurs after both directional particles (21) and positional particles (3) should they occur in the phrase. *Anoo* is incompatible with manner particles (22).

In postposed position the basic meaning of *anoo* is 'again', as in *hoki mai anoo* 'come back again'. But it may also function simply as an intensifier. *Koia anoo*, 'that's it!'; *ko koe anoo* 'you, yourself'; *e tika ana anoo!* 'that's right!'

Study the following examples carefully for the range of meaning of *anoo* in postposed position:

Kaatahi anoo au ka tae mai.
I've just arrived. It's the first time I've come. [Both of these meanings are possible.]

Kaahore anoo ia kia tae mai.
He hasn't arrived yet.

No konei koe? Aae, no konei anoo au.
Are you from here? Yes, I'm from here.

Ka tahuna te whare ki te ahi, me nga taangata anoo i roto.
The house was burnt, and the people inside too.

Me koe na anoo toona aahua.
He looks just like you.

He tikanga anoo no te taane, he tikanga anoo no te wahine.
Men have their ways, and women have their ways.

He kootuku pea teenaa manu? Ehara! He kootuku anoo te kootuku.
Perhaps that bird is a white-heron. No, a white-heron's different. (A white-heron is a white-heron.)

Kaahore he waka mooku? He waka anoo.
Is there no canoe for me? There's a canoe alright.

41.2 *Anoo* as a preposed particle

In preposed position *anoo* always occurs phrase initially, and very often sentence initially. Sentence initially it is pronounced *aanoo* by some speakers.

'As if, like' are the basic meanings of *anoo* in preposed position. It is often used in conjunction with *me*, either in the same phrase, or in a following phrase.

Anoo he reo taane, te karanga mai a Hinemoa.
Hinemoa's voice sounded like a man when she called out.

Anoo te kiri me te anuhe tawatawa, te mahi a te kauri.
The burnt kauri-gum tattooing pigment made his skin like the patterned markings of a mackerel. [A good example of the concise, almost cryptic style of classical Maori.]

Anoo ko Koopuu ka puta ake i te pae, nga karu o te maipi a te tangata ra.
The (*paaua*-shell) eyes of the man's *taiaha* (shone) like the evening-star when it appears above the horizon.

E haere mai ana te taniwha, anoo me he pukepuke whenua.
The monster was approaching, as large as a hillock.

42. Numerals

42.1 General

The numerals are a subclass of statives, and, like statives can occur in both verbal and nominal phrases. Note however that the numeral *tahi* 'one' has an alternative form *kotahi* with the meaning 'one unit' or 'one undivided'. *Kotahi rawa te mea i kitea e au* 'I saw only one thing'; *he iwi kotahi taatou* 'we are one people'.

42.2 Counting

In counting numerals may occur without preposed particles thus, *tahi, rua, toru* 'one, two, three', but it is more usual, in classical Maori, to find the inceptive verbal particle used thus, *ka tahi, ka rua, ka toru*. 'Ten' is *kotahi tekau*.

The numbers one to ten are as follows:

tahi, rua, toru, whaa, rima, ono, whitu, waru, iwa, tekau.

42.3 Numerals used with other verbal particles

The use of verbal particles other than *ka* with numerals is best illustrated with examples:

Kia toru nga herengi. Kua toru inaianei.
Let it be three shillings (make it three shillings). There are three now.

E hia nga paaparakauta o teenei taaone? E rima. E hia nga haahi? Kotahi.
How many hotels are there in this town? Five. How many churches? One.

Note that the verbal particle *e* is never used with *tekau* 'ten'. *Tekau nga whare* 'ten houses'.

42.4 Ordinals

Ordinals may be formed by preposing the singular definite article to the numerals, *te tahi* 'the first', *te rua* 'the second' and so on. Alternatively the ordinal prefix *tua-* may be used with the numerals one to nine, as follows: *te tuatahi* 'the first', *te tuarua* 'the second', etc. The ordinal prefix is not used with *tekau*, nor with numbers higher than ten. If an ordinal fills the second nucleus slot in a phrase the *tua-* form will be used: *te ope tuatahi* 'the first battalion'. Note that *tua-* is also used with *hia?* 'how many?'

> *Ko te tuahia teenei o nga hiimene? Ko te tuarua.*
> Which (in order) of the hymns is this? It is the second.

42.5 Predication of numbers

The verbal particle *e* is used when saying how many things there are:

> *Nga waka e whitu. Nga hau e whaa.*
> The seven canoes. The four winds.

> *E waru nga ruuma o te whare nei.*
> This house has eight rooms.

42.6 *Toko-* the human prefix

When speaking of humans the numbers two to nine, and the interrogative *(w)hia?* 'how many?', are prefixed by *toko-* :

> *Tokohia nga tangata? Tokorima.*
> How many people? Five.

42.7 *Taki-* the distributive prefix

To use a numeral distributively *taki-* is prefixed:

> *Kia takirua mai nga kararehe.*
> Let the animals come in by twos.

42.8 Counting above ten

kotahi tekau maa tahi	eleven
kotahi tekau maa rua	twelve
kotahi tekau maa toru	thirteen
kotahi tekau maa whaa	fourteen
kotahi tekau maa rima	fifteen
kotahi tekau maa ono	sixteen
kotahi tekau maa whitu	seventeen
kotahi tekau maa waru	eighteen
kotahi tekau maa iwa	nineteen
e rua tekau	twenty
e rua tekau maa tahi	twenty-one
kotahi rau	one hundred
kotahi mano	one thousand
kotahi mano e waru rau e whaa tekau	
	one thousand eight hundred and forty (1840)

43. *Taua* and *teetahi*

43.1 *Taua*

The retrospective definitive *taua* means 'the aforementioned'. So *taua tangata* may be translated 'the aforementioned man' or simply 'that man'. Like all definitives *taua* forms its plural by dropping the initial *t*, hence *aua taangata* 'those aforementioned men'.

43.2 *Teetahi*

The specifying definitive *teetahi* and its regular plural form *eetahi* may be translated '(a) certain' as in *teeraa teetahi rangatira* 'there (was) a certain chief'. Note that the indefinite article *he* may not follow any of the locative prepositions *ki, i, hei, kei*. In this position *he* is replaced by *teetahi*. Thus *e moohio ana au ki teetahi tohunga*, not **e moohio ana au ki he tohunga*.

43.21 Dialectal note

Teetahi and *eetahi* are replaced by *teetehi* and *eetehi* in the Waikato–Maniapoto dialectal area.

> *Na, teeraa anoo teetahi paa nui onamata, ko Maunga-whau.*
> Now, there was a certain great fortress in days of old named Maunga-whau.

> *Ka rongo teetahi wahine no runga i tc rangi ki tc toa o Taawhaki.*
> A certain woman in the sky heard about Taawhaki's bravery.

> *Na, i eetahi raa ka tupu te whawhai a taua paa ki nga taangata o Aawhitu.*
> Now, at a certain time, warfare broke out between that fortress and the people of Aawhitu.

> *Ka pirau noa iho teetahi taha o te wahine ra, ka tupuria e te tiotio.*
> One side of the woman became rotten and overgrown with barnacles.

44. The locatives *koo, konei, konaa, koraa, reira*

(Examples from this section may be heard on Track 35 of the recordings.)

44.1 *Koo, konei, konaa, koraa, reira*

Koo 'there', *konei* 'here', *konaa* 'there, near you', *koraa* 'there (neither near speaker or hearer), and *reira* 'there, at the place mentioned before' are all locative class bases (16.5).

44.2 *Koo atu* and *koo mai*

Koo atu and *koo mai* refer to the far side and the near side respectively of a place or object.

> *Kei koo atu o Wanganui tooku kaainga; kei koo mai te kaainga o tooku teina.*
> My home is on the far side of Wanganui; my young brother's home is on this side.

44.3 Examples

> *No hea koe? No konei tonu.*
> Where are you from? From right here.

> *Me waiho i konei te mea na.*
> Leave that thing here.

> *Kei hea taku heru? Kei koraa ra.*
> Where is my comb? Over there.

> *Kei koo atu o Whanganui a Whangaehu.*
> Whangaehu is beyond Whanganui.

> *I haere a Tama-te-kapua ki Moehau, aa, ka mate ia ki reira.*
> Tama-te-kapua went to Moehau, and died at that place.

146

Ka haere a Tainui ki Muri-whenua; ka hoki mai i reira ka uu ki Taamaki.
Tainui went to the far north; then she returned from that place to Auckland.

Ko te tono a te Tari Poutaapeta kia whakakorea te ingoa nei, a Te Kawakawa. No konei ka whataa te ingoa nei, a Te Ara-roa ki runga ki Te Kawakawa.
The Post and Telegraph Department ordered that the name Te Kawakawa be deleted. Thereupon the name Te Araroa superseded Te Kawakawa.

Kia ora koutou i runga i nga aahuatanga i hui mai ai taatou ki konei i teenei raa.
Good wishes to you all concerning the matters for which we are assembled here today.

45. Agreement of qualifying bases and manner particles with passives and derived nouns

45.1 Agreement of bases with passives

Any base in the second position in a passive phrase will take the passive termination *-tia* in agreement with the first base in the phrase:

I kainga otatia nga kuumara.
The kumaras were eaten raw.

I tuaina katoatia nga raakau.
All the trees were cut down.

I tanumia oratia a Te Heuheu raatou ko toona iwi.
Te Henheu was buried alive, together with his people.

I koorerotia pukutia e ia ki a Pou te matenga o Tiki.
Tiki's death was revealed secretly by him to Pou.

E kore ia e haere atu kia utua katoatia ra anoo aa koutou nama.
He won't go away until all your debts are paid.

45.2 Agreement of manner particles with passives

Any manner particle (22) in a passive phrase will take the passive termination *-tia*.

I patua rawatia te hoariri.
The enemy was killed outright.

I kawea keetia e ia toona ingoa.
His name was changed by him.

45.3 Agreement of qualifying bases and manner particles with derived nouns

When a derived noun is used as the head of a nucleus followed by a qualifying base, or a manner particle, the qualifying base and the manner particle will take the suffix *-tanga* in agreement with the principle base in the phrase.

Ko tana patunga pukutanga i a au.
His secretly striking me.

Taenga tonutanga atu ka tiimata te koorero.
Immediately after the arrival the talks began.

I te aonga kautanga o te raa ka haere ia.
As soon as day broke he went.

46. *Hoomai, hoatu* and *hoake*

(Examples from this section may be heard on Track 36 of the recordings.)

46.1 Derivation and use

Each of these bases is derived, by the addition of a directional particle, from a root **ho(o)*, which is no longer found as a separate word. The directional particle in these three cases is written as part of the base. In classical Maori *hoomai, hoatu and hoake* can be used passively, but they never take a passive termination. In modern Maori however the forms *hoomaingia* and *hoatungia* are sometimes heard. *Hoomai* means 'give (to the speaker)', *hoatu* means 'give (away)' and sometimes 'put forth, give out, go forth'; *hoake* means 'go on (especially to a place connected with the speaker)'.

46.2 Dialectal note

Whoatu and *whoake* are dialectal variants of *hoatu* and *hoake* which are marked as modern forms by the occurrence of *wh-* before a back vowel, something that does not occur in classical Maori.

46.3 Examples

Ka mea atu a Hotu-rapa, 'Hoomai hoki ki a au!'
Hotu-rapa said, 'Give (it) to me!'

Ka hoatu te taurekareka hei utu mo te wahine.
The slave was given as payment for the woman.

Ka hoatu tana riri!
He gave vent to his anger.

Hoatu! Me waiho maaua i konei!
Go on! Leave us two here.

Hoake taatou ki te whare!
Let us go to the house.

Koia nei te whakataukii mo te mea kite, e ka kitea te taonga makere,
'Kaaore e hoatu e ahau, ta te mea ko te paekura kite a Maahina.'
Here is the proverb which concerns things which are found, as (for example) when something which has been cast away is discovered, 'I won't give it up, because it is the treasure found by Maahina.'

47. The postposed particle *hoki*

(Examples from this section may be heard on Track 37 of the recordings.)

Hoki means 'and, also, too, indeed'. Its use is best learned from examples, but note that it always comes last in a phrase, following all other postposed particles.

Ka mutu te pakanga, ka mau hoki te rongo.
The war ended and peace was declared.

Teenaa hoki teetahi whakataukii . . .
There is another saying . . .

Ka whai atu ra hoki te kupu kanga i muri i a raatou.
And the curse followed them.

Ko wai ra hoki teetahi?
Who else is there?

Ko koe anoo hoki teetahi i reira.
You also were one of those present.

Noou hoki te rangatiratanga, te kaha, me te korooria.
Thine is the kingdom, the power and the glory.

Ka noho ia ki raro, ka poouri hoki ia ki a ia e kataina ana e te iwi.
He sat down, angry within himself too because he was being laughed at by the people.

I te waa i patu ai te taniwha i a Mere, mangu katoa te wai o te awa, poouri kerekere. I mua, he maarama te wai. I mua hoki, paapaku eetahi waahi o te awa. I taua takiwaa he hoohonu katoa.
At the time when the monster killed Mary the water in the river was all black, very dark. Before, the water was clear. And before, parts of the river were shallow, but at that time it was deep everywhere.

48. The structure of the Maori phrase

48.1 The phrase

Phrase = ± preposed periphery + nucleus ± postposed periphery.

The Maori phrase consists of a central nucleus (which is always present) and a preposed and a postposed periphery, either or both of which may be present or absent in a given phrase. Every phrase is either a verbal phrase or a nominal phrase. In the following subsections the structures of the peripheries and the nucleus of verbal and nominal phrases are examined in detail.

48.2 The nucleus of the phrase

Nucleus = + head ± qualifier

The nucleus of any phrase can be regarded as consisting of two structural positions, or slots, the head slot (which must be filled), and the qualifier slot (which may or may not be filled). In the phrase *te raakau roa* 'the tall tree' the head slot is filled by *raakau* 'tree'; the qualifier slot is filled by *roa* 'tall'. In the phrase *te raakau,* only the head slot of the nucleus is filled.

The nucleus head of a phrase may consist of (a) a simple base, as in the above example; (b) a reduplicated base, e.g. *papaki* or *pakipaki; (c)* an expanded base with one or more affixes, e.g. *whakatangihanga, tuawhitu.*

The qualifier slot of a phrase may contain one or more than one of each of (a), (b), and (c) above.

In the phrase *ka patu puku* 'kill secretly' the head and qualifier slots are each filled by a simple base; in *ka patua pukutia* 'killed secretly' both slots are filled by an expanded base; in the phrase *te whakatangitangi piana* 'the piano playing' the head is filled by an expanded and reduplicated base, while the qualifier is a single simple base.

In the following examples, some of which are more complex, the head of each phrase is in square brackets:

48.2

ko te [mahi] kaamura
carpentry

he [whaea] tuuranga whaanau
a classificatory mother

ko te [take] utu taake
the matter of paying taxes

ko te [kamupene] mahi papa tiihore
the veneer-peeling company

he [urutira] taniwha moana nui
a great sea monster's fin

48.3 The preposed periphery of verbal phrases

Preposed periphery of verbal phrases = ± *me* or *e* ± verbal particle

The preposed periphery of a verbal phrase contains two positions, either or both of which may be filled or empty in a particular phrase. The first position is filled by *me* 'if', or in the case when the verbal particle is *ka* 'inceptive', by *e* 'if, when'. The second position may be filled by any verbal particle. In careful speech this position is always filled except in the imperative of bases containing more than two vowels, e.g. *haere!* 'Go!', or when the phrase contains *ana* or *ai* in the postposed periphery as in *haere ana raatou* 'they went on', *Haere mai ki konei noho ai!* 'come here and sit down!'
Verbal phrases with both preposed peripheral slots filled occur in the following sentences:

Ka ora ra pea ahau e ka tuaina ki te moana.
I will escape if I am chopped down in the sea. [Said by Tama-te-kapua when he was running on stilts].

Koia teenei pepeha mo te mea kite, e ka kitea te taonga makere.
Hence this saying about things which are found, when something which has been cast away is discovered.

(For examples with *me* see 49.12 and 53.1.)

48.4 The preposed periphery of nominal phrases

Preposed periphery of nominal phrases = ± preposition ± definitive or article ± *nei* or *na*

There are three positional slots in the preposed periphery of the nominal phrase. Any of the slots may be empty, but either the first or the second slot must be filled in every phrase. The first slot is filled by a preposition (17) which, in addition to its lexical meaning, also indicates the function of the phrase as a whole in the sentence (38). The second slot is filled by a definitive (15.2) or the personal article *a*, or the indefinite article *he*. The third slot is filled by either of the positionals *nei* or *na* but not by *ra*. Following are examples of nominal phrases with their preposed peripheries filled in various ways:

ki te tangata
to the man

ko Pita
Peter

o ta raatou taurekareka
of their slave

me taua nei rangatira
and that chief (who has just been mentioned)

48.5 The postposed periphery

Postposed periphery = ± manner particle ± directional ± positional ± *anoo* ± *hoki* or *ana* or *ai*

The postposed periphery of both verbal and nominal phrases can be considered as one. There are five positions but it is rare to find more than three filled in a particular phrase. None of the positions are obligatorily filled, and many phrases have no postposed periphery at all. Examples follow:

48.5

na te tangata noa atu
belonging to some unknown person

mo te whenua anoo
concerning the land itself

kia oti noa ake ra
was completely finished

kia riro ai hoki
that may also be taken accordingly

no tata noa iho
from very close

e koorero atu nei
is speaking away here

49. Subordinate constituents of complex sentences

(Examples from this section may be heard on Track 38 of the recordings.)

49.1 General

Most of the sentences that have been considered so far were simple sentences that contained just one subject (38.3) and one predicate (4.1, 38.2). A sentence that contains more than one predicate is a complex sentence. A sentence constituent is a structural part of a complex sentence that contains a predicate (clause may be a more familiar term). A complex sentence will contain two or more constituents, one of which is the main constituent while the other constituents are said to be subordinate (or coordinate) with the main constituent.

Consider 'the boy fell down' and 'the boy climbed the tree'. They are both simple sentences. 'The boy may fall down if he climbs the tree' is a complex sentence because it contains two predicates, ' may fall down' and 'climbs the tree'. 'The boy may fall down' is the main constituent, 'if he climbs the tree' is a subordinate constituent.

49.2 Conditional constituents introduced by *me* or *me he mea* 'if'

Me he mea naau te tamaiti, kua moohio koe ki te roanga o toona ingoa.
If the child was yours, you would have known its full name.

Me i haere mai koe inanahi, kua tuutaki taaua.
If you had come yesterday, we would have met.

Me e haere ana koutou, me hari a Pani.
If you are going, take Pani.

Me kaahore koutou e haere ana, me tuku a Pani kia haere.
If you are not going, let Pani go.

Me i kore koe i hoki atu inanahi, kua tuutaki taaua.
If you had not gone back yesterday, we would have met.

Me ka mahi taatou, ka ora; me ka kore taatou e mahi, ka mate.
If we work we will prosper; if we do not work we will perish.

Me kua oti oo mahi, me haere ki te pikitia.
If your work is finished, go to the pictures.

Me kia tere te koowhaki i te kaanga i mua o te ua, ka haere au.
If it is necessary to hurry the picking of the corn before the rain, I will go.

Me kaahore kia tere te koowhaki i te kaanga, ka haere au ki te tangihanga.
If it is not necessary to hurry the picking of the corn, I will go to the tangi.

49.21 Dialectal note

In North Auckland *me he mea* may be contracted to *me he.* On the East Coast the usual contraction of *me he mea* is *me mea.*

49.3 Conditional constituent initiated by *ki te* 'if'

Ki te followed by a universal or a stative base may introduce a constituent which implies future time and uncertainty as to the outcome.

Ki te mutu te ua, e noho ana taatou.
If the rain stops we are staying.

Ki te kore e whiti te raa, e noho ana maatou.
If the sun does not shine we are staying.

Ka mea a Hinemoa, 'ki te tonoa atu he karere ki a Tuutaanekai e kore pea ia e pai mai ki ahau.'
Hinemoa thought, 'If I send a messenger to Tuntaanekai, perhaps he will not like me.'

Ka mea atu a Horowhenua ki oona tuaakana, 'Ki te purutia atu to taatou matua, hohoro mai, kia tiikina atu.'
Horowhenua said to his older brothers, 'If our father is detained hurry back so that he may be fetched.'

49.4 Active, stative and passive relative constituents

Any nominal phrase may be followed by a qualifying verbal constituent relative to it. The subordination of the verbal phrase is indicated by *nei, na, ra,* or *ai. Ai* is used only for past and future time and when the relativised noun is not the subject of the relative clause.

E titiro ana te tangata ki te wahine e tuu mai ra.
The man is looking at the woman standing there.

He taariana te poaka i pupuhi ai taku matua.
The pig my father shot was a boar.

E moohio ana au ki teenei tangata e haere mai nei.
I know this man who is coming this way.

Ko teewhea te kaakahu, i whatua na e koe?
Which is the cloak woven by you?

Kei whea te ngahere, i puuhia ai teenei poaka?
Where is the bush in which this pig was killed?

Kei koraa ra! Kei te maunga e tuu mai ra.
Over there! On the mountain standing over there.

Ko wai te tangata, e poka nei i te poaka?
Who is the man butchering the pig?

Ko ia te matua o nga tamariki e maatakitaki mai nei.
He is the father of the children who are watching.

49.5 Actor emphatic relative constituents

An actor emphatic construction (24) using *maana* and *naana* for all persons and numbers may be used as a subordinate constituent relative to, and expanding, a sentence which is already complete in sense.

Ko wai te taurekareka, naana nei i tapahi nga waea o te taiapa?
Who was the rascal who cut the fence wires?

Kei hea te puuru, naana nei i whai a Tamahae?
Where is the bull that chased Tamahae?

Kua haere kee nga kaimahi, naana nei i mahi te hei?
The labourers who did the work on the hay have already gone.

I te ata, ka oho nga tamariki, naana nei i tohatoha nga hei.
In the morning the children who spread the hay got up.

Ko koe te tohunga, maana e hanga te whare.
You are the expert who will build the house.

Ko wai maa nga taangata, maana e too te waka ki te wai?
Who are the men who will drag the canoe to the water?

49.6 Relative constituents with T-class possessive

A T-class possessive (14) used disjunctively (i.e. as the nucleus of a phrase) may introduce a relative constituent, as in the following examples:

Kei konei tooku hoa, taau i paatai mai na.
Here is my friend about whom you asked.

Ka mea atu te matua ki tana tamaahine, 'Ko wai taau e pai ai o nga rangatira nei? Maau e whiriwhiri taau e pai ai!' Whakautua ana e te tamaahine, 'Me waiho i taau e pai ai.'
The father said to his daughter, 'Which one of these chiefs do you like? Choose the one you like.' The daughter replied, 'Let it be the one you like.'

49.7 Nominal relative constituents with *naana, noona, maana, moona*

The possessives *naana, noona, maana, moona* may be used for all persons and numbers to introduce a relative constituent, as in the following examples:

Ko wai te iwi, noona te whenua?
What is the name of the tribe which owns the land?

Kei te moohio au ki te tangata, moona te whare na.
I know the man who that house is for.

Ko te Atua, naana nei nga mea katoa.
God, who made all things.

50. Explanatory predicates to stative sentences

A stative sentence such as *kua pau te paraaoa* 'the bread has all been consumed' or *kua pau te paraaoa i te kurii* 'the bread has all been consumed by the dog' may be expanded by the addition of a universal base preceded by the singular definite article: *kua pau te paraaoa te kai* 'the bread has all been consumed (by eating)' or *kua pau te paraaoa i te kurii te kai* 'the bread has all been consumed by the dog (by eating)'.

If the actor in the sentence has not been expressed by a comment after the stative as in the last example above, it may be expressed by an agentive comment after the pseudo-predicate as in *kua pau te paraaoa te kai e te kurii* 'the bread has all been consumed (by eating) by the dog'.

> *Kua mau koe.*
> You are held fast.

> *Kua mau koe te here.*
> You are held fast (by being bound).

> *Kua mau koe i a au te here.*
> You are held fast by me (by being bound).

> *Kua mau koe te here e au.*
> You are held fast (by being bound) by me.

51. Reflexive-intensive pronouns and possessive pronouns

Any pronoun or possessive pronoun, and indeed all personal class bases, may be made reflexive, or intensive by postposing either *anoo* or *ake*. Intensiveness, but not reflexiveness, may also be indicated by *tonu*:

Ka kii atu a Apakura, 'Na wai koe?' Ka kii mai a Whakatau, 'Naau anoo ra ahau.'
Apakura said, 'Whose child are you?' and Whakatau answered, 'I am your own child.'

Ka kii a Whakatau, 'Me au nei koia te aahua?' Ka mea atu taua tangata nei, 'Aae, me koe na anoo te aahua. Ko koe tonu pea.'
Whakatau said, 'Was (his) appearance then like me?' That fellow replied, 'Yes, just like you. Perhaps it was really you.'

Moea to tuahine. Kia riri, ka riri ki a koorua anoo.
Marry your cousin, then when you quarrel you quarrel only with yourselves.

Naau anoo i kawe mai i a koe?
Did you bring yourself here (did you come of your own accord)?

E kore e rite ki tana ake kai, tino kai, tino maakona.
It will not be like his own food (food obtained by himself), good eating, and satisfying.

52. Days, weeks, months and years

52.1 Days of the week

Wiki 'week' and *raa* or *rangi* 'day' are nouns. The days of the week are nouns, taking the singular definite article *te*, or some other definitive:

Mane 'Monday'

Tuurei 'Tuesday'

Wenerei 'Wednesday'

Taaite 'Thursday'

Parairei 'Friday'

Haatarei 'Saturday' *(Raa Horoi* is an alternative form for Saturday)

Raa Tapu 'Sunday'

52.2 Months of the year

Marama 'month' is a noun. The months of the year are personals, taking the personal article *a* like any personal name:

Haanuere 'January'

Pepuere 'February'

Maaehe 'March'

Aaperira 'April'

Mei 'May'

Hune 'June'

Huurae 'July'

Aakuhata 'August'

Hepetema 'September'

Oketopa 'October'

Noema 'November'

Tiihema 'December'

52.3 The years

Tau 'year' is a noun. Particular years are usually given in full, e.g. *'te tau kotahi mano, e iwa rau, e ono tekau maa whitu'* 'nineteen sixty-seven'. Occasionally the century will be omitted: *i te tau e ono tekau maa whitu* 'in sixty-seven'.

52.4 The seasons and special days

The seasons and such special days as Christmas, New Year, are nouns or noun phrases:

Kooanga 'spring'
Raumati 'summer'
Ngahuru 'autumn'
Hootoke (or *Makariri*) 'winter'
Kirihimete 'Christmas'
Tau Hoou (or *Niu Ia*) 'New Year'
huri tau 'birthday, anniversary'

52.5 Examples

Ko te marama o Oketopa teenei.
This is the month of October.

Ko te Wenerei teenei, te rua o Haanuere.
This is Wednesday, the second of January.

Ko te ata o te Taaite teenei, te toru o Tiihema.
This is the morning of Thursday, the third of December.

Kei a Hepetema te tiimatanga o te whaanau o te tuuii, aa, ko te marama whakamutunga ko Maaehe. E rua nga wiki me te haawhe ka paopao nga heeki.
September is the month when the hatching of tuis begins, and it ends in March. The eggs hatch after two and a half weeks.

52.5

Ka tiimata te mahi a te kiore i te ngahuru, i te marama o Aaperira. Tiimata mai i a Aaperira, aa, tae noa ki te marama o Huurae, ka mutu. E whaa marama ka mutu katoa te mahi.

Rat-hunting begins in the autumn, starting in April and ending in July. The whole thing takes four months.

I tiimata te koorero i te waru o nga raa o Pepuere.

The story began on the eighth day of February.

Nga tamariki kaahore anoo kia rima nga tau.

The children who are not yet five years old.

No te tau kotahi mano, e iwa rau maa whitu teenei haerenga ooku. I te ahiahi o te raa o te Kirihimete ka tae maatou ki Te Whaaiti. E rua oo maa-tou raa atu i Rotorua ki Te Whaaiti. Kotahi anoo te raa i Te Whaaiti ki Rua-taahuna. Kotahi tooku raa i whakangaa ai ki reira.

This journey of mine took place in 1907. On the evening of Christmas Day we reached Te Whaaiti. We had taken two days from Rotorua to Te Whaaiti. One more day from Te Whaaiti to Rua-taahuna. I stayed one day resting at that place.

53. More about conditional constituents: 'if' and 'when'

53.1 *Me* meaning 'if'

Me i tahuri taua iwi ki te whawhai ki a Tama maa kua mate noa iho.
If that tribe had turned to fighting Tama and the others, they would have been completely defeated.

Me i noho anoo a Ngaatoro maa i Maketuu, me i kaua te haere ki Moehau, kiihai i wera a Te Arawa.
If Ngaatoro and his people had settled at Maketuu, and if the journey to Moehau had not taken place, Te Arawa would not have been burned.

Me i haere mai koe inanahi kua tuutaki taaua.
If you had come yesterday, we would have met.

Me e haere ana koutou ki Ahuriri me hari a Pani.
If you are going to Napier, better bring Pani.

Me kua oti oo mahi me haere ki te pikitia.
If your chores are finished, go to the pictures.

Me kua tatuu te take me haere nga mahi.
If the matter is decided, get on with the business.

53.2 *Ki te, ki te mea* and *me he mea* meaning 'if'

Ki te or *ki te mea* beginning a sentence may be translated by 'if'. Note that uncertainty is implied. *Me he mea* may also be translated 'if' but it usually implies that the contrary to the condition expressed is known to be the fact. *Me he mea* is often shortened in fast speech to *me he* or *me mea:*

Me he mea kua hinga te raakau, kua kati te huarahi.
If the tree had fallen (but it hasn't), the road would be blocked.

Ki te kore koe e whakaatu mai, e kore ahau e maatau.
If you don't explain, I won't understand.

Me he mea kaahore ahau e noho ana i konei, kaahore he tangata hei hoa moou.

If I were not living here (but I am), there would be no one to be your friend.

Ki te kata koutou i a au i te mea kaatahi anoo au ka tomo atu ki roto, ka mate rawa au, mate rawa atu; engari ki te ngaro rawa au ki roto, puta noa i te waha, ka ora ahau, ka mate a Hine-nui-te-poo.

If you laugh at me just as I am entering, I will be killed, killed immediately; but if I enter completely, and come out from her mouth, then I will live and Hine-nui-te-poo will die.

53.3 *Ana* and *ina* meaning 'if and when'

These two forms appear to be in free variation, both referring to a point in future time when something will happen, but, since it is the future, implying some uncertainty as well. 'When', 'if' and sometimes 'if and when', are appropriate translations:

Ina haere mai koe aapoopoo me heke i taku kaainga.
If (or when) you come tomorrow, get off at my place.

Ina kore koe e haere mai ka haere au ki te hii.
If you don't come, I will go fishing.

E hia, e hia nga punua kararehe e mau ana i te tuna nei, ana heke iho ki te inu.
Great numbers of young animals are seized by that eel when they go down to drink.

Kia mahara ki eenei tikanga ana haere ki te moana ki te mahi kai, hii ika raanei.
Remember these customs when you go to the sea to find food, or to fish.

Kia tuupato taaua, ana hoki mai a te ahiahi.
Let us be careful when we come back in the evening.

53.4 *E* or *e ka* . . . meaning 'if and when'

E whiti koe ki raawaahi, me haere tonu atu koe.
When you reach the other side keep straight on.

Koia teenei pepeha mo te mea kite, e ka kitea te taonga makere.
Hence this saying concerning something found, when something which
has been cast away is discovered.

Kaatahi au ka whakatika ki te whaikoorero e ka tae mai te ope a Mea.
Then (for the first time) I will get up and make a speech when So-and-so's
party arrives.

Kei riri mai koia koe ki a au e ka whaakii atu au ki a koe.
Now don't get angry with me when I tell you.

54. A brief guide to pronunciation

54.1 General

It is not possible to illustrate in writing the exact pronunciation of the sounds of a language; only the human voice can do that, and sound-recordings have been prepared to accompany this course. The best that can be done here, for those who do not have access to the recordings or to some one who speaks Maori, is to liken Maori sounds to their nearest equivalents in English as it is spoken in New Zealand.

54.2 Vowels

There are five vowel sounds, each of which may be said short or long. A long vowel is twice as long as a short vowel in the same position in a word. In *Complete English–Maori Dictionary, Selected Readings in Maori,* and *Let's Learn Maori* all long vowels are written as double vowels. In Williams's *A Dictionary of the Maori Language* the citation forms mark long vowels with a macron.

> Pronounce short *a*, as in *manu,* like *u* in 'nut'.
> Pronounce long *aa,* as in *maanu,* like *a* in 'Chicago'.
> Pronounce short *i*, as in *pipi,* like *i* in 'pit'.
> Pronounce long *ii,* as in *piipii,* like *ee* in 'peep'.
> Pronounce short *e*, as in *peke,* like *e* in 'peck' or 'ferry'.
> Pronounce long *ee,* as in *peeke,* like *ai* in 'pair' or in 'fairy'.
> Pronounce short *o*, as in *hoko,* like *or* in 'report'.
> Pronounce long *oo,* as in *kookoo,* like *ore* in 'pore'.
> Pronounce short *u*, as in *putu,* like *u* in 'put'.
> Pronounce long *uu,* as in *puutu,* like *oo* in 'moon'.

54.3 Diphthongs

Any pair of different vowels is called a diphthong. Maori diphthongs retain the quality of the second vowel quite clearly and most of them are not matched at all closely by anything in English.

Pronounce *ei,* as in *hei,* like *ay* in 'hay'.
Pronounce *ae,* as in *hae,* like *igh* in 'high'.
Pronounce *ai,* as in *hai,* like *ighi* in 'sighing', or *ye-ee* in 'goodbye-ee'.
Pronounce *ao,* as in *kao,* like *ow* in 'how'.
Pronounce *au,* as in *kau,* like *ou* in the BBC pronunciation of 'house'.
Pronounce *ou,* as in *kou,* like *ow,* in 'low'.
Pronounce *ea,* as in *kea,* to rhyme with 'mare'.
Pronounce *ia,* as in *kia,* to rhyme with 'beer'.
Pronounce *ua,* as in *pua,* to rhyme with 'sewer'.
Pronounce *oa,* as in *poa,* to rhyme with 'drawer'.
Pronounce *ei,* as in *kei,* like *ayee,* in 'payee'.
Pronounce *eo,* as in *reo,* as in 'fellow', 'jello', leaving out the *l.*
Pronounce *eu,* as in *heu,* as in 'bet two', leaving out the *tt.*
Pronounce *oi* like *oy* in 'boy'.
Pronounce *oe* as in cortex, leaving out the *t.*
Pronounce *ie* as in *kie,* like *ie* in 'fiesta'.
Pronounce *io* as in *tio,* like *io* in 'Rio Grande'.
Pronounce *iu* as in *piu* like *ew* in 'pew'.

54.4 Consonants

Only three consonants need be discussed. The others are pronounced approximately as in English.

Pronounce *wh* as in 'whale' (not 'wail'), or as *f.* Either is correct.
Pronounce *ng* as in 'singer', never as in 'finger'.
Pronounce *r* as in the Oxford pronunciation of 'very'.

54.5 Word stress

Every base has a word stress which is placed according to the following rules. The rules must be applied in the order in which they are given below. First, however, we must note that the stress must never occur more than four vowels from the end of the word, so in any word containing more than four vowels we consider only the last four. The ordered rules are as follows:

1. Stress the first double vowel, if there is one: e.g. *Máata, papáa, káapene, matáa, kaumáatua, páakehaa*
2. If there is no double vowel stress the first non-final diphthong (a diphthong is defined as any cluster of two non-identical vowels): e.g. *Karáuria, tamáiti, wáiata, Háuturu, táuranga.*
3. If there is no double vowel and no non-final diphthong stress the first vowel which is not more than four vowels from the end of the word: e.g. *híkipene, kánikani, wáhine, tángata, támariki, márae, Oomárumutu, témepara.*
4. If a written word contains more than four vowels the rules are applied again, counting leftwards from the fifth vowel from the end. Most such words are proper names (in which case hyphenating them may be appropriate) or loanwords: *Pámupúria, wíkitóoria, Túu-matáuenga, karáitiána, Páarémoremo, káarámuramu, Páraparáaumu, Kóhimáramara, kóowháiwhai, Ngáaruawáahia, Túurangawáewae.*

54.6 Phrase stress

Maori speakers run their words together interspersed with brief pauses. Such pauses always occur at the end of a grammatical phrase (1.1). The stretch between one pause and another is called an intonation contour. In slow speech each intonation contour may be only one phrase long but in fast speech several phrases may be spoken as one intonation contour. Each contour has a peak of intonation which is heard as the most prominent point in the phrase. This intonation peak is called phrase stress.

In sentence-final contours the phrase stress falls on the last base in the contour and in accordance with the rules for word stress (54.5). In a sentences final contour the pitch of the voice fall (except in questions and exclamations).

In non-final contours, however, the pitch is held up or rises to the end of the contour and the phrase stress falls on the last syllable that contains more than one vowel.

In the following examples the syllable under phrase stress is capitalised:

Ko te rangaTIra, o teenei MArae.

Ko te maRAE, o teenei RAngatira.

He aataaHUA, te marae of teenei KAAInga.

Ko te marae of teenei KAAInga, he aaTAAhua.

Index and vocabulary

Note that, in italicised Maori words only, *wh* and *ng* are treated as single symbols alphabetised after *n* and *w* respectively.

Def.	Definitive	Part.	Particle
Der.	Derived	Pre.	Preposed
L	Locative class base	Post.	Postposed
N	Noun class base	S	Stative class base
Nuc.	Nucleus	Sv	verb subclass of statives
P	Personal class base	Vb	Verb, verbal

A. (l) Pre. part., proper article 2.3, 4.4, 10.2, 35. (2) Pre. part., dominant possession, of 13.1–4, 17.

Aa. And, after a time

Aa. Pre. part., possessive particle, plural of *taa*, the . . . of.

Aae. Yes.

Aahua. N. Appearance, form.

Aakarana. L. Auckland.

Aakona. Passive of *ako* q.v

Aakonga. Der. N. Pupil

Aaku. Def., 1st person singular dominant T-class possessive plural items possessed, my 14.1-2.

Aakuhata. P. August.

Aana. Def., 3rd person singular dominant T-class possessive, plural items possessed, his, her 14.1-2.

Aanoo. See *anoo.*

Aaperira. P. April.

Aapoopoo. L. Tomorrow.

Aaporo. N. Apple.

Aarani. N. Orange.

Aata. Unclassified base occurring only as the first base in compound phrases, intensifying the meaning of the second base. *Aata titiro.* Look carefully. *Aata kite.* See clearly. *Aata haere.* Go slowly, carefully.

Aatuahaa. S. Beautiful, handsome.

Aau. Def., 2nd person singular dominant T-class possessive, plural items possessed, your 14.1–2.

Aawangawanga. S. Anxious, anxiety.

Aawhina-tia. Help, assist.

Action-actor sentences 5.1.

Active (verbal) sentences. Any sentence containing an active universal base 5.1, 6.2, 6.3.

Active universal bases 7.1.

Actor. That which performs an action; of sentence 7.1; emphatic 24; as focus 24.

Adjective 16.1.

Affixes 16.1.

Agent. That which performs the action in a passive sentence.

Agentive particle *e* 7.1; comment 7.1.

Aha-tia. What? *I ahatia koe?* What was done to you? *Aha koa.* Although.

Ahi. N. Fire.

Ahiahi. S. Evening, afternoon.

Ai. Post. part. See 34.2, 49.4.

Ake. Post. part., directional, upwards 51.

Ako-na. Learn. *Aakonga.* Pupil.

Aku. Def., 1st person singular neuter T-class possessive, plural items possessed, my 14.1–2.

Amo-hia. Carry, on shoulder.

Amuamu-tia. Grumble, protest.

Ana. (1) Def., 3rd person singular dominant neuter T-class possessive, plural items possessed, his, her 14.1–2. (2) Pre. vb. part., punctative tense 8.2, 53.3. (3) Post. vb. part., continuative 36.

Anake. Post. part. Alone, only.

Anoo. (1) Post. part., again 41.1, 51. (2) also *annoo.* Interjection. As if, like 37.14, 41.2.

Anuhe tawatawa. Markings on the skin of a mackerel 41.2.

Ao ake. Next day.

Ao-hia. Day, as opposed to night. *Ao ake anoo te raa.* Next day.

Aonga ake. Next day.

Aotearoa. L. New Zealand (especially the North Island).

Apposition 38.7, 49. Items in apposition are serving identical functions in the sentence.

Ara. (1) N. Road, path, way. (2) S. Awake, arise.

Ariki. High or paramount chief.

Aroha-ina, aroha-tia. Love, pity, affection, sympathy.

Article, definite *te, nga, -ee,* 2.2; indefinite *he* 2.1; personal *a* 2.3.

Aspect (of verbal phrases). A grammatical term which refers to the nature, rather than the time of an action or state, e.g. inceptive, continuative, perfect (completed) aspects.

Ata. S. Morning.

Atapoo. S. Early dawn.

Ata-tuu. After sunrise.

Ate. N. Anatomically the liver, but figuratively the seat of the emotions, hence heart, and the object of the emotions, hence darling.

Atu. Post. part., directional away from speaker 21.3.

Au. (1) N. Current. (2) Personal pronoun, I, me.

Aua. Def. Those, aforementioned 15.2.

(Plural of *taua* q.v.)

Auahi. N. Smoke.

Awa. N. River.

Awatea. S. Broad daylight.

Awau. Personal pronoun. Dialectal variation of *au* 9.5.

Balanced nominal sentences 4.

Base classes 16.

Bases. Those words which express lexical meaning and fill the nucleus position in phrases. All words which are not particles are bases 1.2.

Biposed particles. Biposed particles such as *nei,* 15.5, and *anoo* 41 can occur both in the preposed or the postposed periphery of a phrase.

Case 9.1.

Causative prefix. See under *whaka-.*

Comment. The constituent of a sentence marked by an initiating particle *ki, i, hei, kei, e, na, no, ma, mo,* but not itself initiating the sentence 1.2, 6.1, 38.4.

Comment, agentive 7.1, instrumental comment with *ki* 32.25.

Conditional constructions 53; *me* meaning 'if, when' 53.3; *e* or *ka* meaning 'if and when' 53.4.

Conjunctive phrases 38.5.

Constituents, subordinate 49; conditional constituents introduced by *me* or *me he mea* 'if'; conditional comment initiated by *ki te* 'if'; active, stative and passive subordinate constituents 49.4; actor emphatic subordinate constituents 49.5; subordinate constituents with T-class possessives 49.6; nominal subordinate constituents with *naana, noona, maana, moona* 49.7.

Continuous actor emphatic 24.4.

Continuous tense. See Imperfect (continuous) tense.

Definite article 2.2, 12.1 15.2, 16.1.

Definite nominal phrase, is any phrase which begins with any definitive 2.21, 15.2.

Definitives. Any word which includes any form of the definite article, singular or plural, is a definitive. All definitives begin with *t*, which is identified as the singular definite article, and all definitives indicate plural number by loss of this *t*-. 3, 14.1, 15.

Definitives in Williams's grammar and dictionary 16.1.

Derived. A derived noun or other part of speech is one which has been changed, by a grammatical process, from some other part of speech. In English examples would be, 'song' a noun derived from the verb 'sing', and 'strength' a noun derived from the adjective 'strong'.

Derived nouns 13.1, 27, used possessively 27.6.

Derived universals 28.

Desiderative tense verbal particle 8.2, 8.3, 34.

Dialect, dialectal variation 5.41, 9.5, 11.7, 30.4, 36.2, 43.21, 46.2.

Directional particles *mai, atu, iho ake* 21.

Dominant possession 13.

Dual number in pronouns 9.1.

E. (1) Pre. part., agentive particle 7.1. (2) Pre. part., if, when 48.3. (3) Pre. vb. part., non-past tense 8.2. *E . . . ana.* Continuous tense 8.2, 30.1.

Ea. Sv. Requited, avenged, paid, settled

Eastern dialect area 30.41.

Eenei. Def., these, near speaker 3.

Eeraa. Def., those, yonder 3.

Eetahi. Def. Some, certain 15.2.

Eewhea? Def. Which ones? 15.2.

Ehara. Negative; *ehara . . . i* 25.1; *ehara ma, mo, na, no* 25.32.

Exclusive 1st person pronouns 9.3

First Lessons in Maori 16.1.

Focus. The non-verbal constituent of a sentence which either begins the sentence, or itself begins with *ko* (or both) 1.2, 38.3.

Focus particle. *Ko* 4.3, 4.4, 38.3

Future tense, affirmative and negative 20.5.

Gender 9.1.

Gloss. That aspect of the meaning of a word or utterance which is used to identify it (perhaps only for a particular occasion). A gloss does not pretend to cover the complete meaning of a word or other linguistic item 1.2.

Goal of sentence 7.1; possessor goal of sentence 13.1.

Grammar, traditional 16.1

Grammatical meaning 16.1.

Haahi. N. Church.

Haamama. S. Be open, gaping, especially of the mouth.

Haamutana. Hamilton.

Haanuere. P. January.

Haaora. N. Hour.

Haapai-nga. Lift.

Haapuku. N. A kind of fish, groper.

Haatarei. N. Saturday.

Haehae-a. Slash, lacerate.

Haere-a. Go. *Haere mai.* Come here. *Haere atu.* Go away.

Hahae. S. Be jealous (also *hae, puuhae*).

Hai. Locative preposition (lectal form) 11.5, = *hei.*

Haika. N. Anchor.

Haina-tia. Sign.

Haka-a. Haka, a war-dance with vigorous actions, and rhythmically shouted words.

Hanga. N. Thing.

Hanga-ia. Build, construct.

Hao-a. To fish with a net, to surround.

Hapuu. N. Subtribe.

Harapaki. Join battle.

Hari-a. Carry, bring.

Hariruu-tia. Shake hands.

Hau. S. Wind; *hauhau.* Cold air, fresh air.

He. Pre. part., indefinite article. A, an, some 2.1.

Hee. S. Fault, sin, wrong.

Hea (whea)? L. Where?

Heke-a. Descend, go down, flow down etc.

Heeki. N. Egg.

Hei. (1) Pre. part., locative particle, future position 11.5, 12.1, 17. (2) N. Hay.

Hemo. S. Die.

Heo(t)i (anoo). Interjection. Accordingly, as a result, and so it turned out 37.21.

Hepetema. P. September.

Here-a. Tie up, bind.

Herehere. Prisoner.

Heramana. N. Sailor.

Herengi. S. Shilling.

Hia, whia? L. How many?

Hiahia-tia. Desire, want.

Hiakai. S. Hungry.

Hii-a. Fish (with a line).

Hiira. N. Shield.

Hikipene. Sixpence.

Hikohiko. Flash repeatedly, as lightning.

Hiku. N. Tail, of fish or reptile.

Hinga. S. Fallen, as of a tree.

Hipi. N. Sheep.

Hoa. N. Friend, spouse, companion, mate; *Hoariri.* Enemy.

Hoake. Idiom. Set forth, go 46.

Hoani. P. Boy's name (John).

Hoariri. Enemy.

Hoatu. N. Give (away) 46.

Hoe-a. Paddle, as a canoe.

Hohoro. S. Quick, speedy.

Hoiho. N. Horse.

Hoki. Post. part., and, also, too 47.

Hoki-a. Return.

Hoko-na. Buy, sell, trade.

Hoohaa. S. Weary, bored, tired of, sick of.

Hoohonu. S. Deep.

Hoomai. U. Give (towards speaker) 46.

Hoopane. N. Saucepan, pot.

Hooro. N. Hall.

Hootoke. N. Winter

Hoou. S. New.

Horo, hohoro. S. Hurry.

Horoi-a. Wash. *Raa horoi.* Saturday.

Horo-mia. Swallow.

Horomona. P. Solomon.

Horowai. P. Personal name.

Hotu. S. Sob.

Hua. (1) N. Fruit. (2) N. Shoe (3) *Huu. S.* Bubble up, as of a spring, boiling water.

Huhu. Large white grub which lives in decayed trees.

Hui-a. Assemble, meet. *Huinga.* Meeting.

Huka. N. Snow, sugar.

Hunaonga. S. Son-in-law, daughter-in-law.

Hune. P. June.

Hungawai. S. Father-in-law, mother-in-law.

Huri-hia. Turn.

Huru-a. Gird round.

Hutukawa. = Pohutukawa. N. A kind of tree. *Metrosideros excelsa.*

Huu. N. Shoe, boot.

Huurae. P. July.

I. (1) Pre. part., locative particle with broad nneaning of 'past position' or simply connective' 6.1, 6.3, 10.2, 11.4, 17.33, 38.4; *i te* pseudo-verbal past continuous tense 30; after active universals not connoting motion 32.21; after statives 32.33. (2) Pre. vb. part., past tense 8.

Ia. P. He, she, him, her

Iaari. N. Yard.

Idioms 12.4

If. See 49.2, 53.

Iho. Post. part., directional, downwards.

Ika. N. Fish.

Imperative, with universals 19; intonation 19.1; weak imperative with *me* 19.5; imperative with bodyparts 19.3; affirmative with statives 33.1; negative with statives 33.2; negative with universals 20.7.

Imperfect (continuous) tense. *E. . . ana* 8.2, 8.3.

Ina. (1) = *Ana.* Pre. part., punctative tense marker 8.2, 53.3. (2) Interjection 37.32.

Inaianei (also *aianei*). L. Today, now.

Inanahi. L. Yesterday.

Inapoo. L. Last night.

Inceptive tense with *ka* 8.2, 20.6. Denotes beginning of a new action or state.

Inclusive 1st person pronouns 9.3.

Indefinite article 2.1, 12.1.

Indefinite phrase. A nominal phrase containing the indefinite article.

Infinitive 6.21.

Infixed reduplication 40.4.

Ingoa-tia. Name, to name.

Interjections 37.

Interjectory phrases 37.2.

Intonation contour. A single span of intonation, often coinciding with the grammatical phrase, and always containing one most prominent syllable, which is said to bear the phrase stress *(q.v.)* 1.1.

Inu-mia. Drink.

Iri. S. Hanging, suspended.

Iwa. S. Nine.

Iwi. N. Tribe, people, bone.

Ka. Pre. verb. part., inceptive tense marker. Pronunciation of 5.3, 8.2, 20.6.

Kaahaki-na. Snatch away, carry off.

Kaahore. Not, no 20.2, 20.4.

Kaahore . . . i. 25.2.

Kaainga. N. Village, home.

Kaakahu-ria. Garment, put on (of clothes).

Kaamura. N. Carpenter.

Kaanga. N. Maize, corn.

Kaapata. N. Cupboard.

Kaapene. N. Captain.

Kare. N. Breaking waves, surf.

Kaatahi. Interjection. Then. *Kaa tahi anoo.*

Then for the first time, at last, just 37.12.

Kaawana. N. Governor.

Kaawanatanga. N. Government, officialdom.

Kaawhe. N. Calf.

Kaha. S. Strong, strength, powerful.

Kai = kei. Locative preposition (dialectal) 11.7.

Kaikoomako. N. *Pennantia corymbosa*, the wood best suited to making fire by the traditional fire-plough method.

Kaimahi. N. Worker.

Kai-nga. Eat, food.

Kaitoa! Interjection. Serves you right! 37.18.

Kakau. N. Handle.

Kama. S. Quick.

Kamo. N. Eye.

Kamapene. N. Company.

Kanataraka. Contract, contracting.

Kanga-a. Curse.

Kanikani-tia. Dance.

Kanohi. N. Eye, face.

Kapu. N. Cup.

Karaka. N. Clock.

Karamui-a. Swarm on.

Karanga-tia. Call.

Kararehe. N. Animal, beast.

Karauriu. A personal name.

Karere. N. Messenger.

Karu. N. Eye.

Kata-ina. Laugh.

Kati. Sv. Closed, blocked, cut off.

Katikati-hia. Nibble.

Katoa. N. All, every.

Kato-hia. Cut, as of flowers.

Kau. N. Cow.

Kaua. Negative imperative 20.7.

Kaukau, kau-ria. Bathe, swim.

Kaumaatua-tia. Respected elder, leader. Adult.

Kauri. N. *Agathis australis.* Tree sp.

Kau-ria. Swim.

Kawe-a. Carry.

Kee. Post. part., of manner, otherness 22.4.

Keekee. N. Armpit.

Kei. (1) Pre. part., locative particle, present position 11.3, 12.1, 17. *Kei te* pseudo verbal continuous present tense 30.2. (2) Pre. vb. part., warning, do not . . . lest 8.2, 29, 33.2.

Kereruu. N. Pigeon, especially native pigeon.

Kete. N. Basket made of flax, kit.

Ki. Pre. part., locative particle with basic meaning of 'motion towards' 6.1, 6.2, 11.2, 12.1, 16.1, 17.33, 32.21, 32.23, 32.24, 38.4.

Kia. Pre. verb. part., desiderative, may it be 8.2.

Kii-a. Say, speak.

Kiihai. Past negative 20.3.

Kiko. N. Flesh.

Kimo. Wink; *kimokimo.* Wink frequently, blink; *kikimo.* Close the eyes firmly.

Kino. S. Evil, bad, degraded.

Kino-ngia (ki). Dislike, hate.

Kiore. N. Rat.

Kiri. N. Skin.

Kirihimete. N. Christmas.

Kiriimi. N. Cream.

Kite-a. See, find, discover.

Ko. Pre. part., focus particle 4.3, 4.4, 17. 1, 17.2, 17.34, 38.31.

Koa. (1) S. Glad, rejoicing, happy. (2) Post. part., of manner, intensive 22.7.

Koata. N. Quarter.

Koe. P. 2nd person singular pronoun, you 9.3.

Kohi-a. Gather.

Koia. Interjection. Indeed, it is so. Also *koinei, koinaa, koiraa.* See 37.22.

Komenga. Der. N. Munching.

Komiti. N. Committee.

Konaa. L. There, near you 44.

Konei. L. Here, near me 44.

Koo. L. There 44.

Kooanga. N. Spring (season).

Koo(w)hatu. N. Stone.

Koohuru-tia. Murder.

Koopuu. P. The planet Venus, as a morning star.

Koorari. N. Flower-stalk of flax.

Koorero-tia. Talk, speak, story, speech.

Koorua. P. 2nd person dual pronoun, you two 9.2, 9.4.

Kootiro. N. Girl.

Kootou. P. East Coast form of 2nd person plural pronoun, you all 9.5.

Kootaku. N. White heron.

Kooura. Crayfish.

Koowhaki-na. Strip, pick, as of corn.

Koraa. L. There, yonder 44.

Kore. Negative 20.5.

Korokoro. N. Throat.

Korooria. N. Glory.

Kotahi. N. One.

Koti. N. Coat.

Kourua. P. North Auckland form of 2nd person dual pronoun, you two 9.5.

Koutou. P. 2nd person plural pronoun, you all 9.2, 9.4.

Kua. Pre. vb. part., perfect tense 8.

Kuia-tia. Elderly woman; become old, of a woman.

Kukuti. Pass. *kuutia.* Pinch, nip.

Kupenga. N. Net.

Kupu. N. Word, including both single word, and saying or aphorism.

Kura. N. (1) Treasure, traditionally red plumes. (2) School, also *whare kura.*

Kuramaahita. N. Schoolmaster.

Kurii. S. Dog, act like a dog.

Kuti-ngia, kuti-a. Shear, cut, as with scissors.

Kuuhaa N. Thigh.

Kuumara. N. Sweet-potato, kumara.

Kuuware. S. Ignorant.

Local nouns 16.2.

Locative particles *ki, i, kei, hei* 11, 12.2

Locatives, locative class bases. Any base which immediately follows the locative particle *ki* 12.1, 16.5.

Maa. And. 42.8.

Maa. Plural.

Ma. (1) Pre. part., dominant unachieved possession, for 17, 18. (2) 'by way of' 18.32.

Maaehe. P. March.

Maaha. S. many.

Maahunga. N. Head.

Maaia. S. (1) Be brave. (2) Fellow, brave.

Maakona. Sv. Satisfied, replete with food.

Maana. 3rd person singular dominant M-class possessive, for him/her.

Maangere. S. Lazy.

Maania. N. Plain, plateau.

Maanu. Sv. Afloat.

Maaori. Native, indigenous. *Wai maaori* freshwater

Maarama. S. Clear, light. Also a girl's name.

Maaroo. S. Hard, stiff; *maarooroo* S. Somewhat hard, stiff.

Maatakitaki. Look at, inspect, watch.

Maatakitaki-tia. Look at, inspect, stare at.

Maatau-ria. Know.

Maatenga. N. Head.

Maatou. P. 1st person exclusive plural pronoun, speaker and others but not the person spoken to, we, us 9.1, 9.2, 9.3.

Maatua. See *matua*.

Maaua. P. 1st person exclusive dual pronoun, speaker and someone else other than person spoken to 9.1, 9.2, 9.3.

Mahana. S. Warm.

Mahara-tia. Remember, recall.

Mahi-a. Work, do, deed.

Mahue. Sv. Be left behind, abandoned.

Mai. Post. part., directional, motion towards, hither 21.2.

Maipi. N. A spearlike weapon similar to a *taiaha*.

Maka-ia. Cast, throw away.

Makariri. S. Cold, winter.

Makere. Sv. Fall, be dropped.

Mana. S. Power, prestige.

Manawa. N. Heart, breath. *Ma-nawa-nui*. S. Patient, steadfast.

Mane. N. Monday.

Mangu. S. Black.

Mania. N. Plain, flat country.

Manner particles *rawa, tonu, kee, noa, pea* 22.

Mano. S. Thousand, indefinitely large number.

Manu. N. Bird.

Manuhiri. N. Guest, visitor.

Manuwhiri = *manuhiri*.

Marae. N. Meeting ground, courtyard, place of assembly.

Marama. N. Month, moon.

Maranga. S. Get up, arise. *Ma-ranga-tia*. Get up, arise.

Maringi. S. Be spilt, spill.

Maro. N. Kilt.

Mass nouns, Maori equivalents of 2.1.

Mata. N. Eye.

Mataa. N. Flint.

Mataku. S. Frightened, afraid.

Matapihi. N. Window.

Matau. (1) N. Right (side). (2) N. Fish-hook

Mate. (1) S. Sick, defeated, dead. (2) *mate-a* desire, want, need; *matemate*. To die in numbers, be sickly.

Matua. Parent, father. *Matua wahine* mother; *mautua*. Plural of *matua*.

Mau. S. Be caught, held fast; *mau-ria*. Take hold of, seize.

Maui. N. Left.

Maunga. N. Mountain.

Me. (1) Pre. verb. part., prescriptive 8.2. (2) Pre. part. if, when 48., 53.1.

Mea-tia. (1) As a noun this word means 'thing'; as a verb it may mean 'say, think, do, decide'. (2) *Mea*. Personal. So-and-so, what's his name?

Mei. P. May.

Mema. N. Member.

Meneti. N. Minute.

Mere. (1) N. Greenstone club. (2) P. Mary

Mimiti. Be diminished, dried up.

Miraka-tia. Milk.

Mo. Pre. part., subordinate unachieved possession, for, concerning 17, 18.

Moana. N. Sea, ocean.

Moe-a. Sleep, marry.

Mokopuna. S. Grandchild.

Moni. N. Money.

Moohio-tia. Know, be aware of.

Mookena. P. Personal name (Morgan), usually a male.

Moona. 3rd personal singular subordinate M-class possessive, for him/her, concerning him/her 18.4.

Motokea. N. Car, automobile.

Motu-hia. Island, sever, cut off.

Mua. L. Front, fore, before.

Muri. L. Behind, rear, after.

Mutu. Sv. Ended, finished, cut off.

Na. (1) Pre. part., dominant achieved possession, belonging to, by, from 17, 18; *na reira,* therefore 18.22. (2) Interjection. Now, then 37.11 (3) Postposed positional particle indicating proximity to or connection with the hearer 3, 15.1.

Naawai. Interjection. After a time 37.31.

Naihi. N. Knife.

Nanakia. N. Fierce, rascally.

Narrative style with *ana* 36.3.

Negative of verbal sentences 20, formulae 20; transforms of nominal and pseudo-verbal sentences 25.

Nei. Postposed positional particle indicating proximity to the speaker, in space or time 3, 15.1.

Neuter verbs 16.1.

Neutral T-class possessives 15.4.

Niu Ia. New Year.

No. Pre. part., subordinate achieved posses-

sion, belonging to, from 17, 18; *no reira,* therefore 18.22; *no te* and its various meanings 39.

Noa. Post. part., of manner, without restriction 22.5.

Nohinohi. S. Small.

Noho-ia. Sit, live, dwell. *Noho-a-tinana* be present in the flesh, as opposed to being spiritually present, *naho-a-wairua.*

Nominal (non-verbal) phrase, see under Phrase.

Nominal sentence. Any sentence which does not contain a verbal phrase 4.

Nominal sentence, negative transforms of 25.

Non-initial phrase. One which is not at the beginning of the sentence.

Non-past (present and future) verbal particle *e* 8.2, 8.3.

Nooema. P. November.

North Auckland 30.42.

Noun. Any word which can take a definite article but cannot occur as the nucleus of a verbal phrase 16.2.

Noun transformed to universals 28.

Nucleus. The central part of the Maori phrase containing the base of bases, and carrying the lexical meaning 1.2, 15.1, 16.1, 17.2, 48.2.

Nui. S. Big, great, numerous; *nunui.* Plural of *nui.*

Numerals 42; counting 42.2; with verbal particles 42.3; ordinals 42.4; predication of 42.5; with human prefix 42.6; distributive 42.7; above ten 42.8.

Nga. Pre. part., plural definite article, the 2.2.

Ngaati-Porou 30.42.

Ngahere. N. Forest, bush.

Ngahuru. N. Autumn.

Ngaki-a. Cultivate.

Ngaro. (1) Sv. Be lost, destroyed, out of sight.

(2) N. House-fly.

Ngaru. N. Wave.

Ngongoro. S. Snoring sound, to snore.

Nguha. S. Fierce, fierceness.

O. Pre. part, subordinate possessive particle, of 13.1–4, 17.

Of 13.

Oho-kia. Wake up, get up.

Oka-ina. Stab, butcher-knife.

Oketopa. P. October.

Oma-kia. Run.

Onamata. L. Of yore.

Oneone. N. Earth, soil.

Ono. S. Six.

Oo. Pre. part., possessive particle plural 14.1.

Ooku. Pre. part., 1st person singular subordinate T-class possessive signifying plural items possessed, my 14.2, 14.3.

Oona. Pre. part., 3rd person singular subordinate T-class possessive signifying plural items possessed, his, her, 14.2, 14.3.

Oou. Pre. part., 2nd person singular subordinate T-class possessive signifying plural items possessed, your 14.2, 14.3.

Ope. N. Party, company, often but not always a warparty.

Ora. S. Be well, healthy, alive, escaped; *oranga.* N. Survivor, remnant.

Oti. Sv. Completed, finished.

Paa. S. Be struck, blocked, hit.

Paamu. N. Farm. *Kaimahi paamu.* Farmer.

Paapaka. N. Crab.

Paapaku. S. Shallow.

Paaparakauta. N. Hotel, public-house.

Paatai-ngia. Ask, question.

Paaua. N. Paua (abalone); hence spinner made from iridescent shell of same.

Pae-a. Place crosswise, cast ashore, anything which is horizontally crosswise such as a bird-perch, the horizon, a barrier; *paepae.* N. Threshhold, doorstep.

Pahi. N. Bus.

Pai. S. Good. *papai.* Plural of *pai.*

Paipa. N. Pipe.

Paipera. N. Bible.

Paka. P. A boy's name.

Pakanga-tia. War, battle, fight.

Pakeke. S. Old, age, adult.

Paki-a. To pat; *pakipaki-a,* pat frequently, clap; *papaki,* pass; *paaki-a,* slap.

Pakuu. S. Report, as of a gun, explode.

Pango. S. Black; *papango.* S. Blackish.

Pani. P. A personal name, usually a girl.

Paoka. N. Fork.

Paopoo. Hatch, of birds.

Papa. N. A flat surface; *Papa tiihore.* Veneer peeled from logs.

Papaki, pass; *paakia,* slap.

Paraaoa. N. Bread, flour.

Paradigm. A set of particles which will substitute one for another in most or all environments. Members of a paradigm are usually incompatible, that is, no more than one member of the paradigm may occur in the same phrase. Examples of paradigms are the Verbal Particles (8) and the Manner Particles (22).

Parairei. N. Friday.

Paraikete. N. Blanket.

Paremete. N. Parliament.

Pari. N. Cliff.

Partial reduplication 40.2.

Particles. Those words which express grammatical meanings and relationships. Every particle in the language is discussed at some point in the grammar 1.2.

Particles 16.1; preposed 16.1; postposed 16.1.

Parts of speech 16; in Maori according to traditional grammars 16.1.

Paru. S. Dirty.

Passives. A passive base is one which has a passive suffix; a passive sentence or other construction is one which contains a passive verbal phrase 7.0.

Passive, shapes of suffix 7.31; passive transformation 7.1; actor (agent) of passive sentence 7.1; passive forms with long vowels
7.2; passive-imperative 19.3.

Past tense verbal particle 8.2, 8.3.

Patu-a. Strike, kill, club.

Pau. Sv. Exhausted, used up, finished, all
gone.

Pea. Post. part., perhaps 22.6.

Peewhea-tia? How, in what manner ?

Peka. N. Branch.

Pene. N. Pen. *Pene-raakau.* Pencil.

Pepa. N. Paper.

Pepeha. N. Saying, aphorism proverb.

Pepuere. P. February.

Pereti. N. Plate.

Perfect tense; verbal particle 8.2, 8.3,
affirmative and negative 20.4.

Periphery. The marginal portions of the
phrase containing particles, and carrying
the grammatical meaning 1.2,16.1.

Periphery, preposed 8.2, preposed periphery
of nominal phrases 48.4

Periphery, postposed 48.5

Personal class base. Personal names and the
names of things which are personified, the
names of the months, the interrogative
pronoun *wai?,* and all personal pronouns
are personal class bases 5.4, 11.6, 16.1,
16.6.

Personal names. See Personal noun.

Personal noun. The name of a person, or any
animal or object which is personified by a
personal name 2.3.

Personal pronouns. See pronouns.

Phrase 1; as pause unit 1.1; as intonation
contour 1.1; grammar of 1.2; compound
4.3; nucleus of 16.1; periphery of 16.1;
preposed peripheral slot of 16.1; postposed
peripheral slot of 16.1; nominal (non-
|verbal) phrase 15.1, 16.1; phrase stress
1.1, 54.6; verbal phrases 16.1, 16.5;

alteration of order 20; complex 31;
structure of 48.

Phrase stress. See under Phrase.

Pia. N. Beer.

Piirangi-tia. Desire, want, wish for.

Piki. (1) N. Feather, plume. (2) *piki-tia.* Climb,
ascend.

Pikitia. N. Picture, movie.

Piko. S. Bent, bowed down.

Pipi. N. Cockles, or other bivalve shellfish.

Pirau. S. Rotten, putrid.

Piriote. N. Billiards.

Piro. S. Smell, scent (usually unpleasant).

Pita. P. Peter.

Place names 12.3.

Plural of pronouns 9.1; of definitives 15.1.

Poaka. N. Pig.

Poihaakena. L. Sydney (from Port Jackson).

Poka-ia. Eviscerate, make an incision.

Pooneke. L. (From Port Nick) Wellington.

Pootae-a. Hat, be crowned.

Poouri. S. Dark (opposite of light), sad,
gloomy, angry.

Poowhiri-tia. Welcome, greet.

Positional particles. *Nei, na, ra* 3, 15.1.

Possession, dominant and subordinate 13,14;
neutralisation of dominant and subordinate
possession 29.

Possessives, particles *a, o,* 15.1; pronouns
14.2; T-class possessives 14.2.

Postposed. Occurring after the phrase
nucleus, not before it 1.2.

Postposed particle. A particle which occurs
in the postposed periphery *q.v.*

Postposed periphery. That portion of a phrase
which follows the nucleus 1.2, 16.1.

Poti. N. Boat.

Poto. Sv. All consumed, used up, exhausted.

Pou-a. Post, be driven in as a post; *pou-
tokomanawa.* N. The main post in a
meeting-house.

Pourewa. Stage, platform.

Poutaapeta. Post-office.

Predicate. The verbal constituent of a verbal sentence 1.2, 38.2. As relative clause 49.4. Of a nominal sentence 4.5.

Preposed periphery. That portion of a phrase which precedes the nucleus 1.2, 15.1, 16.1.

Prepositions 17; prepositional phrase 17.3.

Prescriptive tense verbal particle *me* 8.2, 8.1.

Pronominal. Pertaining to pronouns.

Pronouns 9, 10; dual and plural number 9.2; inclusive and exclusive 1st person 9.3; table of 9.4; dialectal variation 9.5; as subject 10.1; after *ki, i, hei, kei* 10.2, 11.5; as part of definitive 15.1; N-class possessive 18.4; M-class possessive 18.4; reflexive-intensive 51; T-class possessive 14.2.

Pronunciation, of *ma, mo, na, no* 18.1; of proper article *a* 35.2.

Proper article *a* 5.4; pronunciation of before *ia* and *koe* 10.3, 11.6, 16.1.

Pseudo-predicate. An action stated in a nominal (not a verbal) construction 50.

Pseudo-verbal sentences, negative transforms of 25; pseudo-verbal continuous tense 30; goals of universals and statives 32.24.

Pua. N. Flower.

Puare. S. Open, hollow

Pueru. N. Garment.

Puhi. N. Feather plume.

Puhipuhi. Adorned with plumes.

Pupahi, pass. *puuhia.* Shoot.

Purei-tia. Play.

Pukapaka-tia. Book, letter, document

Puke, pukepuke. N. Hill.

Puku. (1) *N.* Belly, stomach. (2) In the qualifier slot of the nucleus this base carries the meaning 'secretly, silently etc.' *Haere paku* 'go in secret', *noho paku* 'remain quiet' or go without food.

Puna. N. Spring (of water).

Punctative/conditional verbal particle 8.2, 8.3.

Pune. N. Spoon.

Punua. N. Young, of animals only.

Pupuhi, puuhia. Shoot, blow (of wind).

Pupuri, pass. *puritia* or *purutia.* Hold fast, cling.

Purei. Play. *purei kaari.* Play cards.

Puruma-tia. Broom, sweep.

Purupuru, pass. *purua.* Stuff up, block up.

Puta. S. Appear, go forth.

Puu. (1) *N.* Gun. (2) A clump, as of rushes, reeds.

Puuhaa. N. Sow-thistle.

Puuhae. S. Jealous, jealousy.

Puuhia. Passive of *pupuhi* q.v.

Puuru. N. Bull.

Puutake. N. Cause, root, basis.

Puu-toorino. N. Flute.

Qualifying base. A base which describes, defines or modifies the meaning of the base it follows.

Ra. Postposed positional particle indicating distance from the speaker in space or time 3,15.1.

Raakau. N. Tree, wood, stick, weapon.

Raawaru. N. A kind of fish. *Parapercis colias,* rock cod.

Rahi. S. Big, important.

Raatou. P. 3rd person plural pronouns, they all 9.4.

Raaua. P. 3rd person dual pronoun, they two 9.2, 9.4.

Raawaahi = taawaahi. L. The far side of an expanse such as a sea, river, plain.

Raka. S. Lock.

Rangatira. S. Chief, gentleman, person of high rank, boss.

Rangi. N. Sky, heaven, day.

Rapu-a. Seek.

Raro. L. Under, underneath, below.

Rau. (1) *N.* Leaf. (2) *S.* Hundred.

Raumati. N. Summer.

Rawa. Post. part., of manner, intensive 22.2.

Rawe-a. Wrap around.

Rea. Spring up, grow.

Reflexive-intensive pronouns 51.

Reka. S. Sweet.

Relative clauses. See 49.3.

Retrospective definitive *taua* 43.

Rewa. Sv. Float, set forth (especially by water).

Rewi. P. Dave.

Reduplication 7.2, 40; complete 40.2; partial 40.3; infixed 40.4.

Reflexive pronouns 21.43.

Reira. L. The aforementioned place, there.

Reo. N. Voice.

Rere. S. Fly, also flee.

Rima. S. Five.

Ringa, ringaringa. N. Hand, arm.

Riri-a. Anger, rage, fight.

Riro. Sv. Taken, acquired, seized, gone.

Rite. S. Like, equal, comparable to, matching.

Roa. S. Long, tall; *roroa.* Plural of *roa*

Roimata. N. Tears.

Rongoa. N. Medicine.

Rongo-hia, whakarongo-hia. (1) Hear, listen, news. (2) *Rongo.* N. Peace.

Rooku. N. Log.

Roto. (1) N. Lake. (2) L. Within, inside.

Rourou. N. Small plate-sized food-basket.

Rua. (1) S. Two, second. (2) N. Hole, pit.

Ruku-hia. Dive, dive for.

Rumaki-na. Disappear, be immersed in water.

Runga. L. Top, above.

Ruuma. N. Room.

Ruupeke. Sv. Be all assembled.

Sentence 1.1; stative sentences 5.2, 6.2, 6.21, 6.31; structure 49.1; expanded sentence defined 49.1

Specifying definitive *teetahi* 43.

Stative class bases. Any base which can be used verbally but not passively is a stative 6.3, 6.31, 13.1, 16.4, 16.5.

Stative class bases, transformed to nouns 28.1, pseudo-verbal goals of 32.24, numeral subclass 42.

Stative sentences 5.2, 6.21, 6.31.

Stress 54.5.

Subject of sentence 38.3.

Subordinate possession 13.

T-class possessives 14.2, 15.2.

Taa. Pre. part,. possessive particle 14.

Taaima. N. Time.

Taaite. N. Thursday.

Taakaro-tia. Play.

Taaku. Pre. part., 1st person singular T-class possessive, my 14.2.

Taamure. N. A kind of fish, snapper.

Taana. Pre. part., 3rd person singular dominant T-class possessive pronoun, his, her 14.2.

Taane. N. Male, husband, man.

Taaone. N. Town.

Taarai-a. Adze out, as a canoe hull.

Taaria. See *tatari.*

Taariana. N. Male animal, stallion, boar.

Taatahi. L. Shore, beach.

Taatou. P. 1st person inclusive plural pronoun, we all 9.2, 9.3, 9.4.

Taau. Pre. part., 2nd person singular dominant T-class possessive pronoun, your 14.2.

Taaua. P. 1st person inclusive dual pronoun, you and I. 9.2, 9.3, 9.4.

Taawaahi. L. The far side, usually of a body of water.

Tae-a. Arrive, achieve.

Taha. S. Side, pass by. *Taha moana.* Seaside.

Tahaa. N. Calabash.

Tahi. S. One.

Tahu-na. Set alight, ignite, burn.

Tahuri. Turn.

Taiaha. N. A fighting staff.

Taiapa. N. Fence.

Taihoa. Interjection. Wait a while! Hang on!

Taitama. Youth, teenager. Plural *taitamariki.* The singular form must refer to a male but the plural term is inclusive of boys and girls.

Taka. S. Fall, fallen, dropped.

Takahi-a. Tread, trample, walk on.

Takai-a. Wrap up, bind.

Take-a. Reason, cause, root, origin.

Takere. N. Hull of a canoe.

Taki-. Pre. nuc. part., distributive 42.7.

Takiwaa. N. Time, space.

Takoto-ria. Lie down.

Taku. Pre. part., 1st person singular neuter possessive, my 14.2.

Tama. N. Son.

Tamaiti. N. Child.

Tamariki. S. Children. Used nominally *tamariki* always takes a plural definitive. Used verbally however it may refer to a singular noun, e.g. i *a au e tamariki ana* 'while I was a child'. cf *tamaiti.*

Tana. Pre. part., 3rd person singular neuter possessive, his, her 14.2.

Tangata-tia. Person, human, mortal, man. *Taangata.* Plural of *tangata.*

Tangi-hia. Weep, lament, sound. *Tangihanga.* Funeral, tangi.

Tango-hia. Take, take hold of.

Taniwha. N. Monster, usually reptilian and often aquatic.

Tanu-mia. Bury.

Taonga. N. Valuable, precious possession.

Tapahi-a. Chop.

Tapu. S. Sacred, prohibited, under ceremonial restriction; *Raa Tapu.* Sunday.

Tapawae. N. Footprint.

Tara. Peak, point, spine.

Tara o te marama. Horn of the moon.

Tarakihi. N. A kind of fish.

Taranaki-Wanganui river area 11.7.

Tari. N. Department, office, secretariat.

Taringa. N. Ear.

Taro ake. Idiom. Shortly afterwards.

Tata. S. Near, close.

Tatari, taaria. Wait for, await.

Tatau. N. Door.

Tatuu. Sv. Settled, confirmed made permanent.

Tau. N. Year, season.

Taua. (1) Def. That (aforementioned). (2) N. War party.

Tauranga. Der. N. Landing place.

Taurekareka. N. Slave.

Tautohe-ngia. Argue, argument.

Tawhiti. N. Distance. Also L. Distant place.

Te. Pre. part., singular definite article, the 2.2; as class marker 2.22.

Teeina. See *teina.*

Teenaa koe, teenaa koorua, teenaa koutou. The most usual form of Maori greeting. It might be translated as Good-day, or How do you do.

Teenei. Def. This.

Teeneti. N. Tent.

Teepu. N. Table.

Teeraa. Def. That, distant from speaker.

Teetahi. Def. A certain, a, an 43.2.

Teewhea? Def. Which?

Teina. N. Sibling, or junior relative of the same sex. *Teeina,* plural of *teina.*

Teitei. S. High, lofty, elevated.

Tekau. N. Ten.

Temepara. Temple.

Tere. S. Swift, fast flow, to sail, school of fish, drift.

Tia. N. Deer.

Tia-ina. Steer.

Tiihema. P. December.

Tiikera. N. Kettle.

Tiikina. Passive of *tiki.* Be fetched.

Tiikiti. N. Ticket.

Tiimata-ria, tiimata-ia. Begin.

Tiitaha. S. Aside, slanting, obliquely.

Tika. S. Straight, correct, true.

Tikanga. N. Custom, way, manner.

Tiki (passive *tiikina*). Fetch.

Tikitiki. Traditional hair-style, with carefully dressed topknot

Tinana. N. Body, physical presence as opposed to spiritual.

Tino. Very.

Tiotio. N. Barnacles.

Tipu-ria = tupu-ria q.v.

Tirohia. See *titiro.*

Titiro, tiro-hia. Look at.

Toa. (1) S. Brave, courageous, warrior. (2) N. Store, shop.

Tohatoha. Spread out, scatter.

Tohe-a. Argue, be stubborn.

Tohunga. S. Adept, expert. Priest, wizard, skilled artisan.

Tokanga. N. Large food-basket.

Toki. N. Axe.

Toko-. Pre. nuc. part., human 42.6.

Tomo-kia. Enter.

Tono-a. Send, demand.

Tonu. Post. part., of manner, continuity 22.3, 51.

Too. (1) Pre. part., possessive particle 14. (2) Pre. part., 2nd person singular neuter T-class possessive, your 14.2.

Tooku. Pre. part., 1st person singular T-class subordinate possessive, my 14.2.

Toona. Pre. part., 3rd person singular subordinate possessive, his, her 14.2.

Toou. Pre. part., 2nd person singular subordinate T-class possessive, your 14.2.

Tope-a. Fell, chop down.

Toro, totoro (passive *torona*). Stretch out, as of the hand. Spread, of a fire.

Toru. S. Three.

Toto. N. Blood. In classical Maori this word always took a plural article, and was not used verbally. In modern Maori it may be used as a universal *toto-ngia.*

Traditional grammars 16.1.

Transforms, negative, of verbal sentences 20.

Transitive verb 16.1.

Tua-. Pre. nuc. part., ordinal 42.4.

Tuahine. S. Sister, female cousin (of male); *tuaahine.* Plural of *tuahine.*

Tuahine. N. Sister of a male. Any female relative of the same generation (male speaking).

Tua-ina. Chow, chop down.

Tuakana. N. Elder sibling of the same sex, brother, sister. Also person of the same sex who is a senior relative of the same generation, a senior cousin; *tuaakana.* Plural of *tuakana.*

Tua-whakarere. L. The far distant past.

Tuhoe–Bay of Plenty area 11.6.

Tuku-a. Release, let go.

Tuna. N. Eel.

Tungaane. N. Brother, speaking from point of view of a sister.

Tupuna. N. Ancestor, grandparent; *tuupuna.* Plural of *tupuna.*

Tupu-ria. Grow, increase.

Turaki-na. Fell a tree by pushing it over.

Ture. N. Law.

Tuu. N. Belt.

Tuuii. N. Tui, parson-bird.

Tuupaapaku. N. Corpse body.

Tuupato. S. Suspicious, wary.

Tuupuna. See *tupuna.*

Tuurei. N. Tuesday.

Tuu-ria. Stand, stop.

Tuuru. N. Seat, chair.

Tuutaki-na. Meet, come up against, close (of door).

Tuutata. S. Close, near.

Tuwhera. S. Be open, gaping.

Ua-ina. Rain.

Uira. N. Lightning

Universal class bases. Any base which can take a passive suffix universal 6.2, 13.1, 16.3, is a passive universal, 7; derived universals 28.

Upoko. N. Head.

Ururoa. N. A kind of shark.

Urutira. N. Dorsal fin.

Uta. L. Inland as opposed to shore, land as opposed to sea.

Uta-ina. Put on board, load, cargo.

Utu-a. Pay, price, money, revenge.

Uu. S. To land, of a vessel.

Uunga. Der. N. Occasion of landing, of a vessel.

Verb 16.1, verb 'to be' 4.1, verb-noun 16.1.

Verbal particles 8; compatibility with base classes 16.1.

Verbal phrase. Any phrase which begins with a verbal particle, or has imperative intonation, or has *ana* or *ai* postposed and no article preposed 1.2, 8, 16.1, 23.2.

Verbal sentences, negative transforms of 20.

Vowels. 54.2.

Waa. N. Time, period of time.

Waahine. See *wahine.*

Waahi. N. Place, part.

Waake. Walk.

Waata-kirihi. N. Watercress.

Wae, waewae. Leg, foot, lower limb.

Waea. N. Wire (also in sense of telegram).

Waenganui. L. Middle, midst. *Waenganui poo.* Midnight.

Waha. N. Mouth.

Waha-a. Carry on back.

Waharoa. N. Main gateway to a fort.

Wahie. N. Firewood.

Wahine-tia. Woman; *Waahine.* Plural of *wahine.*

Waho. L. Outside.

Wai. N. Water, liquid. *Wai maaori.* Fresh water.

Wai? P. Who? whom?

Waiata-tia. Sing, song, chant.

Waiho-tia. Leave, remain.

Waimarie. S. Luck, good-fortune, lucky, fortunate.

Waka. N. Canoe, vehicle.

Ware. N. Commoner, person of low rank.

Waru. S. Eight.

Wau. P. Dialectal variation of 1st person singular pronoun *au* 9.4.

Wehi. S. Fearful, afraid.

Wenerei. N. Wednesday.

Wera. S. Hot; *werawera.* S. Warm.

Western dialect area 30.41.

Wiiwii. Rushes, reeds.

Wiki. N. Week.

Wikitooria. Victory, Victoria.

Williams's *A Dictionary of the Maori Language* 16.1.

Wini. S. Win, be a winner.

Wiwiri. S. Trembling.

Word. That utterance segment which is written between spaces 1.

Whaa. S. Four.

Whaanau. S. (1) Be born. (2) Extended family group.

Whaanau-a-Apanui, Te. The tribe which occupies the Bay of Plenty from Maraenui to Cape Runaway.

Whaangai-tia, whaangai-a. Feed, foster, raise, fosterchild.

Whaea. N. Mother.

Whai, pass. w*haaia.* Pursue, follow; *whaiwhai poaka,* pig hunting.

Whaikoorero-tia. Speak formally, formal speech, oratory.

Whaka-. Pre. nuc. part., causative prefix; prefixed to locatives means 'in the direction of' 28.4

Whakaae-tia. Agree, consent.

Whakaaro-tia. Think, thought.

Whakaatu-ria. Reveal, tell, disclose.

Whakahaere-a. Manage, conduct, lead.

Whakahee-ngia. Disagree, contradict.

Whakairi-a. Suspend, hang up.

Whakairo-hia. Carve, sculpt.

Whakaiti-tia. Belittle, make small.

Whakakino-tia. Debase, make bad.

Whakakite-a. Reveal.

Whakamaa. S. Ashamed, shy, embarassed.

Whakamarumaru-tia. Shady.

Whakamate-a. Kill.

Whakamoohio-tia. Instruct, warn, inform.

Whakamuri-a. Backwards, move backwards.

Whakangaa. Rest, recuperate.

Whakanoho-ia. Set in place, settle on.

Whakaora-tia. Make well, save.

Whakapukepuke-a. Well up, of tears.

Whakapono-ngia. Believe.

Whakarere, pass. *whakareerea.* Cast away, reject.

Whakareri-ngia. Make ready, get ready.

Whakarongo-hia. Listen.

Whakataetae-ngia. Compete for, contest.

Whakatakariri-ngia. Rage, anger.

Whakataki-na. Seek, go to find, meet.

Whakatangitangi-hia. Play, of musical instrument.

Whakatakoto-ria. Lay down, place.

Whakatanakutanga. Der. N. Swallowing.

Whakatapu-a. Sanctify, prohibit.

Whakatata-ngia. Approach, come near.

Whakataukii-tia. Proverb, aphorism, saying.

Whakatika-ngia. Straighten, correct, arise.

Whakatoi-ngia. Tease.

Whakatupu-ria. Rear, grow.

Whakatuu-ria. Set up, erect, build.

Whakautu-a. Repay, answer.

Whara. Sp. Be hurt, wounded, injured.

Whare. N. House. *Whare-nui.* Meeting house.

Whata-a. Lay, place, as on a shelf, hang.

Whati-ia. Break, snap.

Whatitoka. N. Door.

Whatu-a. Weave.

Whawhai-tia. Fight, battle.

Whea (hea)? L. Where?

Wheetero. S. Protrude the tongue as a gesture of ceremonial defiance and/or greeting.

Wheke. N. Octopus.

Whenua. N. Land, country.

Whero. S. Red; *whewhero.* S. Reddish.

Wheua. N. Bone.

Whia, hia? L. How many?

Whio, whiowhio. Whistle.

Whiriwhiri-a. Choose, select.

Whiti-kia. Shine, of sun.

Whitu. S. Seven.

Whiu-a. Whip, punish, fling.

Whoatu = hoatu q.v.